Colección
EMPRENDIMIENTO
Y CRECIMIENTO PERSONAL

Pan House
Casa Editorial

Editorial PanHouse.
www.editorialpanhouse.com

General Editing:
Jonathan Somoza
General Management:
Paola Morales
Editorial Management:
Jorge Rodríguez
Editorial Coordination:
Bárbara Daniela Peña
Spanish Content Editing:
Chiara Flores
Translation:
TIex Global
Proofreading:
Gretchen Martens
Design, cover and layout:
Audra Ramones

ISBN: 978-980-437-357-2
Legal Deposit: DC2024000907

Dr. Bárbara Flores Caballero

LEADERSHIP WITH VISION and HEART

A Practical Guide that Integrates Emotions and Strategies as a Differentiator

PanHouse

TABLE OF CONTENTS

DEDICATION

To my three life mentors Carmen Caballero, Awilda Rodríguez and Carmen Jiménez because you have inspired me with your example to serve others from the heart. I love you.

ACKNOWLEDGMENTS

Luisa De los Ríos, you left me ecstatic with the prologue, thank you very much. Grateful to Gretchen Martens, Celi Marrero, Nilda Rosario, Nivia Pérez, Rubén Hernández, Carmen Jiménez, Eva Ramírez and Dr. Leidy K. Pichardo for their time and for sharing such beautiful words.

To all the university students and leaders from all over the world, you were my inspiration, thank you very much. Dear Saraí González, what a privilege to have you collaborate in this adventure with me! My most sincere gratitude. God, thank you, thank you, thank you for all your blessings, for making another one of my dreams come true and for blessing me with my beloved daughter, Victoria, who is my best teacher. I love you.

My sincere thanks to Miranda, Paola, Chiara, Jonathan, and the entire team at PanHouse Publishing for being part of this very special project.

ABOUT THE AUTHOR

Bárbara Flores Caballero

Puerto Rican author Bárbara Flores Caballero is an associate professor, researcher, writer, international congresswoman, member of the Doctoral Dissertation Committee and contributor to television and radio media. As a specialist in emotional intelligence and educational leadership, she is the founder and host of the podcast *Transforming Knowledge* and her YouTube Channel *Bárbara FloresEI.*

She was the winner of the Latin Podcast Award, 2020 Edition, in the Education category. She is also founder and creator of the *EduLíder* Emotional Leadership Program. She has been part of projects as a writer and speaker at conferences in Costa Rica, Portugal, Argentina, Mexico, Spain, Chile, Dominican Republic, Colombia, Puerto Rico, and the United States, where she has addressed topics on leadership and emotional intelligence.

As a specialist in emotional intelligence and leadership, she has a decade of experience, within her twenty years as a professional in the field of education. She has helped not only children and adolescents, but also different professionals in their training and coaching in leadership and emotional intelligence, both in the educational and business fields.

Her performance as a professional, with more than twenty years of experience is not only limited to Puerto Rico but extends to North Carolina and New York. With a true passion for teaching, Dr. Flores is dedicated to motivating, inspiring, and influencing the future leaders of our society, seeking to generate a genuine impact in the field of educational and business leadership, from a place of emotional intelligence.

Spotify: @TransformingKnowledge
Instagram: @doctorabarbaraflores
Website: barbaraflores.info
Facebook: @BarbaraFloresei
Twitter: @barbarbarafloresei

Saraí González Berríos
Collaborator

Characterized as being a dynamic professional who gets diverse companies in motion to strengthen those mechanisms that lead them to obtain positive results, Saraí González Berríos has more than twenty years of experience in the field of human resources, where she practices her profession with dedication and passion.

As part of her professional career path, she has worked in prestigious companies, impacting diverse industries in areas such as insurance, trade, education, construction, and health. In addition, she has held key strategic positions within her these diverse workplaces. She has taught seminars, lectures and workshops aimed at human resources professionals, management personnel, leaders, and collaborators.

In 2017 she founded Assertive Connections, a Puerto Rican firm dedicated to promoting best practices in the field of human resources, as well as for individuals who occupy, or aspire to occupy, leadership positions. She gave shape to one of the dreams that she had been maturing for five years and, finally, in 2021 launched Assertive Academy.

This initiative consists of an academy that brings together, in one place, a range of educational activities that have been taught for more than a decade. The Academy uses an online platform aimed at professionals in leadership positions and professionals who wish to expand, update, and strengthen their competencies.

FOREWORD

For some time now, I have understood that growing is not only about adding knowledge and experiences. I have understood that relationships play a major role in this process and that ignoring them can be detrimental to my development and plans. Opening my eyes to that truth also meant that it was time to take some unsentimental steps. Without a doubt, I had to do a makeover in the closet of my associations. I had to be severe in this exercise. Not cruel, but vertical, looking to my upward growth. I had to stay loyal to my plans, my principles, my nature, my ideals and my vision of life.

At that moment I had a choking feeling, a feeling of fatigue. It was like listening to constant rain that does not stop and demands you walk through mud. After the "clean-up," not only did this sensation disappear, but I was more relaxed and free to develop new alliances of value, the ones for which a coffee is equivalent to a certificate on your wall. Better yet, when that perception exists in both directions, you and your new ally both experience this. These things are not possible when you have all your mental spaces occupied with people whose time in your life has expired and where you have not yet honored the potential in you by preparing the space for what is yet to come. I invite you to make a mindset shift about this, to make up your mind once and for all and do it: take an inventory of your relationships and purge the ones that don't serve you. You will see the powerful acceleration that your life acquires and you will not believe it.

This preamble has been to tell you in what season the author of this book came into my life. Bárbara's previous publication, *EduLíder Emocional*, which if you have not read it yet, I recommend, was a pleasant surprise in my life as well. Not only did I learn from her strategies, but I also got to know a woman who is passionate about what she does, to the point that she has no reservations about sharing what has cost her many early mornings, exhaustion, and sacrifices. That, without a doubt, captivated me and gave me back confidence in good people, in honest alliances, in the idea that there are men and women with a genuine desire to help others grow, just for the joy of seeing them succeed.

Now Bárbara comes along and does it again! She surpasses her own mark with a complete work, an accurate, precise, and always practical book. A thesis that right before my eyes becomes the irrefutable evidence that what I did one day with my environment was nothing more than the necessary preparation to receive these lessons today. She specializes in the figure of the leader in any context: the workplace, the school or university, the sports team, the church, the fraternity, or club, including an association of residents or even a group of mothers who help out at school. These groups, and many more, will benefit greatly from this treatise.

Life reflections and decisions will accelerate in your brain as the distinctions between IQ, emotional intelligence and social intelligence are revealed to you. Not to mention when you open your eyes to the evidence of how much your leadership measures up to the yardsticks of generations, collaborators, self-analysis and even one of my favorite topics, body language. But you will recover from catatonia as the reading progresses, your future plans are defined and you stand firm in your agenda.

Bárbara will provide you with varied resources to the point of exhaustion. Here you will have a plurality of measuring instruments with which you will be able to maximize your leadership skills to a level you never imagined. I must confess that, in the eyes of a commercially oriented person with pupils in the shape of dollar signs, this book may seem like a bad deal, as it reveals too much and the cancellation of its publication and distribution could surely be proposed.

I confess I might agree! Unless, as I told you in the beginning, you know Dr. Bárbara Flores Caballero to be the personification of an injection of hope in good people. I know she delights in sharing her findings, tools, and bibliographies (so that continuity in your study be a further extension of her project); all for the joy of seeing others grow. That makes her feel as if she is growing alongside you.

The book you are about to read will surprise you, both for what you will discover and for its deep insights. You will have several QR codes that will transport you to links that you can benefit from, because they include strategies that increase the value of this naturally meritorious study and that make you part of a community of individuals who are not satisfied and want more. Metaphorical or parabolic illustrations make timely appearances. They are like strategically placed oases, cleverly and gracefully spaced out to refresh our minds, keep us alert and maintain a high level of comprehension.

At the end of this book, you will see that what started out as a book ends up as a powerful tool enriched with your own annotations. It will hardly join the rest of your books on the shelf at home but rather require its own easily accessible space for frequent reference.

Bárbara, my friend, thank you for the privilege of entrusting the foreword of your work in my hands. I admire your intelligence, but I admire your heart even more. You are the mother goose that relieves me of 71% of my effort when you lead in front of me.

Thank you! God bless your talent, your company, and your family!

To you, the reader, enjoy this book and when that person who should also read it comes to your mind, remember that you will have to give them this book, but not yours, which will already have your thoughts engraved on it and will carry your evolution as an indelible mark.

Happy reading!

I remain of you, a book away.

Luisa De los Ríos

TESTIMONIALS

"Dr. Bárbara Flores Caballero is a leader who manages to empower her subordinates in every project or task she assigns. Her ability to teach coupled with teamwork is, from my perspective, her letter of success.

For her, there is no small challenge or employee and that is why she manages, with all her administrative skills, to enhance every task or challenge she performs; however, she recognizes that her workforce is the best asset for success. She has a high degree of respect for every employee in the company no matter what position they hold. In this way she separates herself from the image of the boss and becomes the leader we want to follow."

Nivia Pérez

Administrative Assistant, COSSMA

"Dr. Flores Caballero has an innate ability to understand the impact of her emotions and those of her supervisees, which helps her generate professional commitment. Her emotional intelligence dominates her leadership success. With this she achieves motivation, knowing that there may be discouragement or frustration in the team.

Her empathetic personality and management of her own emotions, as well as those of her colleagues, saved the difficult ending that was looming over my unfair working condition. She brings together what a leader requires. Her self-knowledge and self-control, qualities that together with her empathy and social skills, allow her to manage her emotions."

Rubén Hernández Rosario

Educator, MA Education, former Dean

"In my career as a publicist and literary consultant I have had the opportunity to work with many wonderful authors, but there are a few who left an indelible mark, as is the case of Dr. Bárbara Flores Caballero.

From our first meeting I knew that she bore witness to what she wrote about emotional intelligence and leadership. That ability to know how to manage relationships and be sensitive to our emotions and those of our fellow man is an intelligence that very few have and that many should practice in order to have better results in their daily lives at a personal and professional level.

Thank you, Bárbara, for the professional that you are, for the legacy that you continue to leave through your books and above all for the impression of love that you leave on everyone who knows you. For our company it is an honor to have a talent such as yourself and to be able to recommend you to so many companies that need to carry this message to raise leaders with impact and emotional intelligence."

Celi Marrero

CEO / CM Events & Media Planners LLC

"Dr. Bárbara Flores Caballero has accustomed us to that easy and direct way of explaining and seeking solutions to situations in our lives. I must confess that, whether I listen to her, watch her or read her, I always find the perfect word in her.

In this third book published by Dr. Flores we continue to enjoy the excellence, and at the same time the simplicity of her advice. Bárbara, I call her by her name because she invites you to that closeness, she is one of the professionals that any communicator wants to have on their team, because she has the ability to transform complex explanations into simple and plain words so that anyone looking for help can understand.

Now, I invite you to make this new success of Dr. Bárbara Flores part of the books that accompany you and be one of your life references."

Nilda Rosario

Entrepreneur and co-host of El Jukeo Mega 97.9 FM

"From the moment I met Dr. Bárbara Flores Caballero at the Directors Leadership Academy, I was impressed with her ability to captivate the audience, given that she was able to fully engage them with emotional intelligence. She was able to introduce the construct of emotional intelligence the group of directors, organized hands-on activities to develop the skills, and then shared strategies for presenting EI to teachers and students.

I was fascinated, not only with her knowledge and skill in EI but also with the way she demonstrated all the skills that an emotionally intelligent person may have. She kept her audience mesmerized, engaged, and requesting a second day to participate with her. There are many people who can talk about EI, but very few can convey this information with the same effect as Bárbara. I was witnessing great andragogy in action! She was able to keep the attention of everyone in that room. She demonstrated with skill and demeanor what great teaching looks like when you use your emotional intelligence skills; it was truly amazing to witness.

After that workshop, I have been able to witness how her books have helped and supported not only leaders, teachers, and college students, they have also helped parents improve their EI skills to communicate more effectively with their children. Dr. Bárbara Flores Caballero can make people see the impact of their EI skills in building better relationships and improving communication. She is remarkable —I look forward to reading her new book!"

Carmen A. Jiménez

Executive Leadership Coach Partner On Point Leadership!, LLC

"Having the pleasure of conversing with Dr. Bárbara Flores Caballero is to immerse yourself in a transformative journey toward self-discovery and authenticity. With her deep knowledge and insight into the world of emotional intelligence, her words and works are invaluable guides to help you navigate the complexities of your emotions and connect with your true self. With her valuable perspective, Dr. Flores inspires you to develop greater emotional awareness and find balance to achieve that confidence that empowers you in all facets of your life in order to achieve your full potential. To meet Bárbara is to remember the essence of my beloved island of enchantment, Puerto Rico, magical, vibrant, kind, with a joyful spirit, celebrating life despite the obstacles, because that is what it is all about, helping to transform the ordinary into a world of possibilities. Thank you for so much, Bárbara!."

Karinna Rojas

General Manager & Principal Advisor Consultank

"Dr. Bárbara Flores Caballero brings such a passion to her work, and this book is an expression of this passion. She lives what she advocates, treating even the most difficult person with kindness and compassion. She brings out the best in everyone she meets, as every good leader should. Bárbara brings her devotion to developing people to her reader. Her advice is straightforward and accessible to managers and novice leaders as well as those with decades of experience. She uses the power of storytelling to illustrate her leadership lessons. Bárbara covers the full range of leadership topics, providing something for every leadership challenge. She engages the reader with many opportunities to self-assess, creating a bridge between theory and practice, and providing the learner with actionable steps to grow. Congratulations to Dr. Bárbara Flores Caballero on her third book! *Abrazos, amiga mía.*"

Gretchen Martens

Author, Publisher, and Leadership Coach

"I met Dr. Bárbara Flores Caballero in Portugal. We both participated in the 1st edition of the 'Leadership Conferences: Add and Grow,' and we had the opportunity to share much more than just the stage. The days we spent together allowed me to discover an extraordinary woman, as wise as she was. She was humble, fun, witty, and always willing to collaborate with enthusiasm and a smile on her face. In her professional aspect, she overflows with passion for what she does; she loves teaching and is very clear about the power of leadership and the influence that a dedicated can generate in her students. And what to say about the lecturer, Bárbara? Well, it's a gift from her to see her in action! Dr. Flores is energetic, motivating, and masterful. So much so that she made us all fall in love with her presentation, and she left her light shining in our hearts and her teachings engraved in our memories."

Eva Ramírez

Editor, writer, and creator of spaces for consciousness

"Dr. Bárbara Flores Caballero has been a colleague and mentor to me since I had the pleasure of meeting her a few years ago at Bronx Community College. I had the joy of working alongside her in the Latino Association and the HSI (Hispanic Serving Institution) committee at Bronx Community College.

As a member of the Latino Association she established a scholarship for students who exhibit emotional intelligence and leadership in their student career. On the HSI committee, we work together to provide guidance and training to our colleagues about the importance of serving our Latino students in an equitable manner.

Dr. Flores Caballero assisted me as a mentor in the doctoral process and in other areas as an administrator. For me, this educator inspires me to move forward, to use emotional intelligence skills in every aspect of my leadership. A woman passionate about education, who strives to see her students excel and achieve their goals, Dr. Bárbara Flores Caballero is an example of Latino pride."

Dr. Leidy K. Pichardo

Director of EOP & Workforce Student Success,
SUNY Rockland Community College, New York

INTRODUCTION

Leadership is not synonymous of domination,
but the art of convincing people to
collaborate to achieve a common goal.
Daniel Goleman

If we look back, we will notice that just a few decades ago many human beings lived in societies that presented a structure of linear thinking, in which challenges were faced in a way that was inclined more towards collectivism. In fact, it could be said that humanity has long been immersed in a system that teaches everyone to think and act in the same way.

However, it is also true that there have been significant advances in all areas of knowledge, including psychology and neuroscience. Nowadays, when we talk about intelligence, we are not only limited to talking about a faculty of our mind that allows us to analyze, reason or learn, but we can also focus on the areas where these processes are carried out.

This is how we can now talk about emotional intelligence (EI) and social intelligence (SI), which do not have to do with the intellectual intelligence (IQ) of each individual, but with aspects such as adaptability to different situations, something that does not depend on the intellect, but on the management of our emotions.

In this sense, one aspect that must be kept in mind is that when a major significant event of great impact occurs worldwide—such as, for example, the pandemic caused by COVID-19 or the war that has resulted from the Russian invasion of Ukraine—no one is fully prepared to experience a crisis. These particular crises, in this case, a health crisis and an economic crisis, can provide us with a new approach capable of transforming the pillars of our lives, as we have seen has happened.

In fact, we can affirm that, just as history was divided into a before and an after Jesus Christ, there is also a before and an after for a crisis. This relates to EI, in how we manage our emotions and take advantage of these critical moments in a positive way. Do we see the glass half full instead of half empty?

Everything has changed! Needs have transformed! So have the ways of doing business! Every person, without a doubt, is different from the way we were before the COVID-19 health crisis, from the way we looked at life, to the way we related to the way we worked, to the way we prioritized finances and other interests. This is a clear and common example to all mankind, we all experienced it, and many people took advantage of it to learn and grow.

Faced with such a changing environment, today, more than ever, organizations have had to face new challenges. What tools does a leader count on to manage all the sudden changes that are occurring in all areas? Are the management models in line with this new change of era?

In the field of business, it is clear that the constant digital transformation has made inroads through the creation of algorithms, the metaverse, big data, artificial intelligence, and remote work, among others. But these changes have also been generated in the more human side. If in the past the important thing was to focus on products, services, and brands to maximize profitability, today the focus is on the people who make up the organization.

However, are organizations really aware of what leadership is all about today? Many of them are, but others not so much. I understand that to be a good leader you need to have a high level of EI and SI. Precisely, this book seeks from this approach to describe this new way of leading, to reinforce each tool for organizational development and the formation of potential leaders, but also to reinforce those who already are leaders, by the strengthening of their EI and SI.

My name is Bárbara Flores Caballero. I was born in Puerto Rico. I am a researcher, writer, author, mentor, and international speaker with more than twenty years of experience in the field of education. I have a Master's degree in Business Administration in Human Resources and a Doctorate in Educational Leadership with a specialization in EI and Leadership.

I have served as Vice President of Planning and Development at Huertas College in Puerto Rico. Currently, I am an Associate Professor at the Bronx Community College, CUNY, in New York. In addition, I am the founder and creator of the *EduLíder* Emotional Leadership Program and winner of the Latin Podcast Award 2020 in the category of Education.

My intention is to share all this knowledge and experience so that you can strengthen your leadership based on EI. Together with Saraí González Berríos, a contributor to this book, she makes available to you from the field of human resources all her experience in the area.

This book is a leadership tool designed for you. Its content is theoretical and practical; at the end of each chapter you will find bullet points, keywords, bibliographical references, and exercises or QR codes to enrich the content. In this way, we would like you to get fully involved with your training and the mastery of the different leadership tools that you will find herein.

Let's get started!

CHAPTER 1:

A TOUR THROUGH THE ERAS OF LEADERSHIP

A leader is one who knows the way, makes the way, and shows the way.

John C. Maxwell

The Lion Goes to War[1]

The lion, king of the jungle, worried because other animals in a bordering area had just declared war on him. However, the lion, a fabulous leader among the rest of the animals, had a plan, so he gathered all his subjects:

"Friends! A neighboring king has just declared war on us. All right, we will defend ourselves. But don't worry, because together we will form the best army."

The lion asked his advisor, the monkey, for help. Between the two of them, they began to organize all the animals to form a powerful army. In this manner, they called on each animal to explain what their mission would be according to the qualities and abilities of each such animal.

"Elephant, come here," said the lion, "you are very strong; you will be very useful to carry all the ammunition. Stones, tree trunks, your strength will be phenomenal and come in handy!"

"Yes!" replied the elephant. "I will carry whatever is necessary!"

"Snake, you will be in charge of spying on the enemy," the lion explained. "You are silent and can sneak in anywhere to find out what their strategy is."

"I love that job!" said the snake.

---

1 Your favorite story (2021). *The lion goes to war.* A fable about leadership for children.

“I need you foxes,” continued the lion., “You are the most cunning of all the animals. I want you to come up with strategies and tactics of assault to win this war.”

”We will think about it right away!” replied the foxes.

”And you bears,” said the lion., “With your strength and agility you can climb the walls when they block our way.”

”It is done!” said the bears.

And just like that, one after another, each animal was given a task. Until the king’s advisor, the monkey, said to the lion:

”Majesty, we have a problem.”

”And what is the problem?” asked the lion.

”We have two animals that seem to be of no use to us. We could make up any excuse to send them home.”

”And what animals are those?” —the lion, intrigued.

”The donkey and the rabbit” answered the monkey. “I don’t think either is of any use to us. The donkey is too dumb, your majesty, and the rabbit is too small and weak.”

”You are wrong” said the lion, somewhat disgruntled. “Listen well: all animals have a function to fulfill and something to contribute. So do the donkey and the rabbit.” And after saying this to the monkey, he called out to both animals.

”Donkey, you will be in charge of calling all the animals to line up when I tell you to. Your voice is even more powerful than mine.”

”Fantastic!” said the donkey.

”And you, rabbit, you are so fast that you are a great help to me in carrying messages back and forth. You will be the messenger; your work is of vital importance.”

The two animals smiled gratefully. The monkey, saddened, bowed his head; he had just received a great lesson from the lion. He was the best leader for a reason, the king of the jungle. Now he was convinced that, together, they would win the war.

What seems to be a defect may well be a virtue.
Only the good leader is capable of seeing it that way.
Estefania Esteban

Eras of Leadership: A General Context

At present, there is a more mature concept of this figure called leader. Before, it was thought that his or her path was solitary, with many pressures and responsibilities on their shoulders, practically a superhero who could save an entire organization. But, as the above story has shown us, the leader cannot succeed alone, but rather needs a team of collaborators, each with an essential role to play in achieving the organization’s objectives.

We only need to take a brief look at the evolutionary line of leadership throughout history to notice how the role of leader has been an imposing figure, even chameleon-like, from less civilized environments to those that are, on the contrary, very civilized, in order to offer solutions to the needs and demands of organizations with very different natures. It is time to begin this journey.

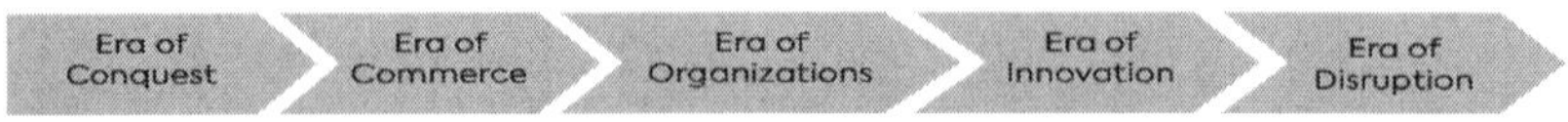

Source: Bárbara Flores Caballero

1. Era of Conquest

If we had to give a name to this first leader, from a chronological point of view, it would be "conqueror," since we are referring to the era of conquest. That leader was characterized by giving security through powerful armies, being a good strategist to negotiate with allies, dominating enemies, invading territories, taking possession of the riches and distributing the spoils of war among their subjects. Their goal was to colonize.

The end and object of conquest
is to avoid doing the same as the vanquished.
Alexander the Great

2. Era of Commerce

The commercial era comes next, wherein the leader had the ability to manufacture and sell; for example, perfumes and wigs in the Middle Ages, whose customers belonged to royalty and nobility. These merchant leaders provided jobs and a standard of living for their followers. Also, they were very skilled in bartering and negotiations, procurement of raw materials, and supplying goods or products.

Trade is the art of buying for three francs what is worth six and selling for six what is worth three.
François Marie Charles Fourier

3. **Era of Organizations**

   Continuing along this path, the figure of the organizational leader emerges and at this moment the sense of belonging begins to develop. This leader is now aware that they have to project the image of efficient and effective leadership, capable of solving the different challenges that arise and directing a work team by providing information to collaborators in order to optimize performance and increase the profitability of the organization.

In this era information is highly valued, because only a few possess it.

Keep in mind that information is power.
Bill Gates

4. Era of Innovation

Following the evolutionary line of leadership, we have a fourth era, that of innovation. This era refers not only to technological advances, but also to the creation of emerging markets. Therefore, the innovative leader recognizes that they must be the first to break paradigms and attract more people; this leader wants to stand out and surpass the competition. This leader demands creativity and excellence from their team, as well as sharing their vision.

If I had asked people what they wanted,
they would have told me a faster horse.
Henry Ford

5. Era of Disruption

And finally, in the fifth era, disruption appears, which in turn, is linked to the concept of breaking the system that teaches everyone to think and act in the same way (i.e., leaving aside the paradigm that everyone thinks alike). In fact, it is young people who are initiating this revolution.

Civilization needs a new operating system;
you are the programmers.
Paul Hawken

It is important to make clear that this system leads to less creative performance, it does not allow you to look outside the box, nor does it allow you to connect with yourself through EI, much less with others.

From a leadership point of view, breaking with this paradigm is a way of saying that a way of thinking should never be imposed. Therefore, the leader in this disruptive era assumes that there is a diversity of opinions and truths.

That diversity causes the value of information to change. Before, information was one of the most valued things in a leader's profile, because only a few people possessed it. Now, in the midst of myriad technological advances, information is within everyone's reach. In addition, constant immediacy prevails, taking into account that it is possible to find any information quickly through millions of channels.

The Internet provides the right information, at the right time, for the right purpose.
Bill Gates

In addition, digital transformation and artificial intelligence also mark a milestone in this disruptive era. In that regard, we must mention the Fourth Industrial Revolution, or Industry 4.0, which comprises automation of industrial processes, optimization of mobility systems, machine learning, blockchain, artificial intelligence, big data, the metaverse, and the digital economy, among others.

However, although organizations and entire sectors still remain immersed in this fourth revolution, the next era is on our doorstep: Industry 5.0. This is characterized not only by technological advancement, but also by a shift in focus from economic value to social value, considering true well-being, instead of focusing on social welfare.

Among its characteristics are personalized manufacturing; the implementation of co-bots or collaborative robots; human empowerment by delegating mechanical, dangerous, and routine tasks to artificial intelligence; speed and quality in the industrial production chain; and something very important, respect for the environment.

In view of these advances and perspectives, the way of doing business and leading has changed completely; consequently, a new profile has been established: leaders and their collaborators must possess technological knowledge and skills, competencies that adapt to this new revolution of Industry 4.0.

So much so that in 2019 Deloitte, the world's largest professional services firm, conducted a survey on how organizations were preparing for the Fourth Industrial Revolution. The report argued that leaders are aware of the new challenges that arise; for example, the inability to work efficiently between different areas or departments, lack of vision, and lack of knowledge of different technologies, among others. The good news was that leaders had the best attitudes to adapt to the changes. Below is the graph of the results obtained:

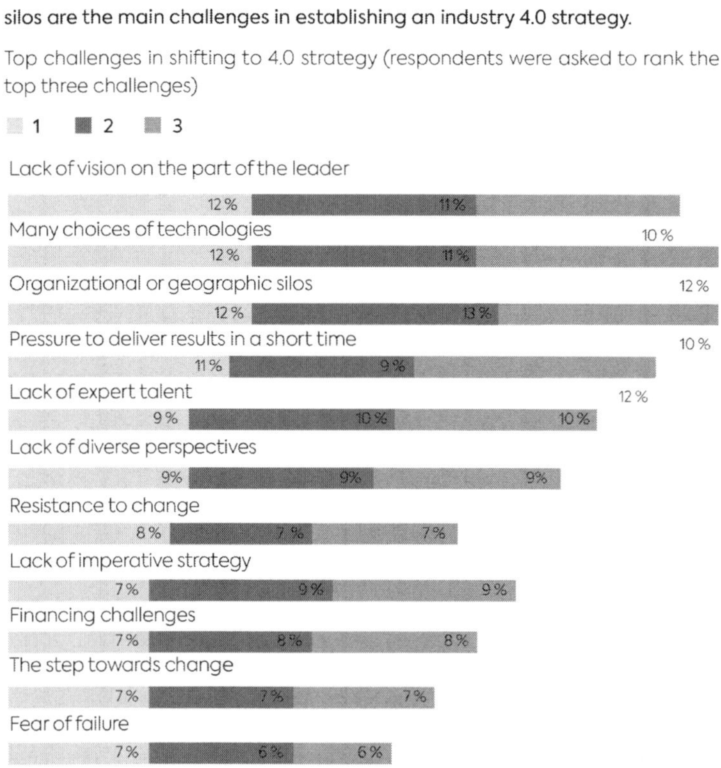

Source: Deloitte Insights (2019)[2]

In short, this report established the importance for organizations to be visionary; that is, to adopt new technologies (i.e., 4.0 Industrial Revolution) with a long-

2 Deloitte (2019). Success personified in the Fourth Industrial Revolution. Four leadership personas for an era of change and uncertainty. Deloitte Insights.

term vision. This entails investing not only in the acquisition of software equipment but also in the training of leaders and partners in order to create competitive advantages, optimize results and maintain organizational stability in the face of crises or changes of era.

On the other hand, it is important that leaders and collaborators are aware that in this disruptive era, not only technical knowledge is required, but also EI; this entails developing empathy, resilience, flexibility, adaptability, and conflict management skills, which I discuss in greater depth in the next chapter.

Further evidence that we are in this the Fourth Industrial Revolution is that older generations, even our parents' generation, never heard of a hybrid workplace. This refers to remote work, that combination between the old way of working in the office and working remotely, from home, with technological tools. In fact, hybrid work is already a reality that is here to stay.

The changes of the recent disruptive era have caused leaders and collaborators to evolve, including an authentic development of their EI and the acquisition of new knowledge and tools, elements that allow them to broaden their vision to face the new demands and challenges.

Although this disruptive era brings many advantages, it is not better than the previous eras in fact, none of them is. Each one developed in a specific stage with particular characteristics; all of them presented advantages and disadvantages. Moreover, without any one of them, the following era would not have been possible and this evolution, which is now possible to observe when reviewing the overall timeline, would not have happened.

Current Context of Leadership

The systematized study of organizational leadership actually began about seven decades ago, standing out today for being presented from a more positive approach. This is crucial, considering that this point of view has an impact on the functioning of organizations, especially with regard to the fulfillment of activities and goals. Therefore, we can say that, without a doubt, leadership has a direct influence on the effectiveness and efficiency of organizations.

Although we have just reviewed the eras of leadership, other clear evidence of leadership evolution can be found in the different research and literature on the subject. Different approaches can be observed in them. From the earlier belief that a leader is not made but is a person who possesses a set of innate qualities; to the leadership understood as a set of behaviors that can be put into practice and executed; to a humanistic vision of leadership proposed in 1978 by James MacGregor Burns in his work *Transforming Leadership*.

The process of evolution of leadership has led to the differentiation between the leader and the manager within business organizations, specifically because it is the leader who innovates and the manager who is in charge of implementing the innovations. It is this new type of leadership that really seeks to respond to current needs, including the various concerns that are generated today; for example, how to maintain motivation in employees and generate commitment from them, in addition to issues such as frequent staff reductions or low profitability, among many others.

This new approach is characterized by understanding leadership as a process that occurs, to a greater or lesser extent and with different features, in each organization based on the social interaction between its different members. In fact, it is a direct consequence of this type of interpersonal relationship, depending on how they are carried out.

The question then arises: Is a leader born or made? There are several research studies that provide insight into this debate, but as Carlos Alsua, professor at the University of Alaska Anchorage and expert in executive leadership, points out: "The leader is born and made… It is a learning process" (*Conexión Esan*, 2011). Indeed, it is possible that a person brings with them natural leadership qualities, but a person may not know everything, there is always something to learn, and that is precisely what I want to show you throughout these pages. I hope we achieve a wonderful symbiosis between leadership and EI to face the challenges of this disruptive era.

Leadership Styles

After having gone through the eras of leadership and understanding the current environment, it is precisely in the organizational era, from the business point of view, that a variety of leadership styles emerge and even coexist. There are many; however, I will take into consideration the most well-known ones.

1. **Autocratic Leadership**

   This leader assumes full responsibility in decision making and may even impose force in order to achieve their objectives. The follower perception is of a superior, competent being, compared to the team, who is treated as subordinates. This leader may even think: "If I am not there, nothing works" or "They are all incompetent."

There is a well-defined hierarchical structure in which power and control are the protagonists. Empathy is not encouraged, much less EI, only the achievement of objectives. This autocratic leader tends to keep the doors of their office closed, thus marking a clear boundary with the work team. Consequently, this leader projects an image of maximum authority, unattainable and unappealable, demanding maximum respect.

I don't care how much my ministers talk,
as long as they do what I tell them to do.
Margaret Thatcher

2. Democratic Leadership

In this case, the leader focuses on offering guidelines; however, before making a decision, this leader consults their collaborators, listens to them and then analyzes each idea or proposal in order to select the option the leader considers most suitable.

This leader has a marked capacity for self-regulation. They are not authoritarian or dictatorial; in fact, this leader supports the team and motivates them to continue their efforts to achieve the organization's goals. This leader proposes, for example, "Tomorrow we will vote to resolve this issue, but I will be the one to make the final decision."

Great leaders get out of the way
to increase their people's self-esteem.
If people believe inthemselves, it's amazing
the things they can accomplish.
Sam Walton

3. Laissez-faire Leadership[3]

In this approach, the leader does not constantly intervene in decision making, but waits for the team to assume responsibility for achieving organizational goals. At no time does the leader delegate, they only set the objectives, assuming a passive role. Nor does this leader support the team; in fact, they provide very little contact. The way of thinking is, "You all get together, I can't meet tomorrow, you decide."

Of course, collaborators must have high performance, commitment, and a qualified profile for this style of leadership to work and obtain satisfactory results.

Leadership is action, not a position.
Donald McGannon

4. Transactional Leadership

As its name indicates, this leadership style is based on transactions or exchange of values or other interests between the leader and their team. This type of leadership consists of delegating a series of tasks or activities with clear guidelines and, depending on the team's effort, performance and results, rewards (e.g., bonuses, recognition, promotion) or sanctions

3 French expression whose meaning is "to allow to do".

of some kind (e.g., reprimands, pay cuts, demotions, termination) are granted.

The transactional leader supervises each phase of the process. Because transactional leadership is based on task accomplishment, this style can work very well in critical or decisive moments for an organization. This leader thinks, "I need materials for my division that you have, and I can trade with you what I have that you need."

None of us got to where we are alone. Whether the help we received was obvious or subtle, acknowledging someone's help is a big part of understanding the importance of saying thank you.
Harvey Mackay

5. **Transformational Leadership**
   Mentioned above, transformational leadership is characterized by inspiration and motivation on the part of the leader, and from the leader to their team. Transformational leadership provides vision and a sense of mission; promotes trust and intellectual stimulation; and offers personalized attention, guidance and advice to their collaborators.

Likewise, the transformational leader fosters an environment of values, ethics, and high standards. Moreover, this leader has a way of thinking and acting that can be understood in the following phrase: "I have noticed that you are unfocused, you have been late these days. Tell me, how can I help you, are you going through a personal situation, how can the organization help you?"

The best discovery of all time is that a person can transform his or her future just by changing their attitude.
Oprah Winfrey

These different leadership styles are not a set of straitjackets; a leader does not necessarily have to be tied to a single style. In fact, the leader can adjust a style perfectly to a particular situation they are facing; for example, getting to know those collaborators who are part of their team or connecting with other people from other areas or organizations. As I mentioned earlier, the relationship between a leader and their team is crucial.

Intergenerational Leadership

Currently, within the organizational world, it is possible for up to four generations to coexist: baby boomers (1943-1960), Generation X (1961-1980), millennials or Generation Y (1981-2000) and Generation Z or nexters (born after 2001). Why is this important in leadership? Each of these age groups has its own characteristics, motivations, expectations, even habits, behavior patterns and attitudes.

How could a leader connect with their team and not take this factor into consideration? Yes, indeed, it is not enough just to know the variety of leadership styles. In order to overcome the different challenges that arise, it is necessary, first of all, to overcome the difficulties caused by these generational differences, taking advantage, like the lion, of the strengths of each group.

One of the keys to leadership is to recognize that everyone has gifts and talents. A good leader will learn to bring those gifts together toward the same goal.
Benjamin Carson

This type of leadership is aware of generational factors; therefore, leaders will seek to establish agreements between leaders belonging to different generations (Chileset al., 2010). The worldviews of these age groups are different, there is undeniable diversity in this regard; however, this could offer advantages when it comes to carrying out processes that encourage innovation and bring about greater motivation. Intergenerational leadership, more than a style, is a competency.

According to a standard proposed by the Spanish foundation *Observatorio Generación y Talento*, together with the European University of Madrid (2018), it is necessary for an intergenerational leader to possess five fundamental characteristics.

The leader must be:

1. A good communicator
2. Responsible
3. Empathetic
4. Collaborative
5. An integrator of all collaborators

Situational Leadership

After understanding that a team is made up of people from different generations, professions; from a situational leadership point of view it is understood that a leader must adapt to their collaborators. This approach was proposed by Paul Hersey and Ken Blanchard in 1969; however, it is Blanchard's model that I will take as a reference, considering that it is based on maintaining a balance between two different behaviors on the part of the leader:

1. As a manager: defines tasks, schedules, and controls results
2. Being Supportive: focuses on the development of the team, encourages participation when making decisions and supports the group

From these two behaviors, four leadership styles are produced:

1. Control: a higher percentage of directive behavior and a low percentage of supportive behavior
2. Supervision: high percentage of both behaviors

3. Counseling: high level of supportive behavior and low level of directive behavior
4. Delegation: low level of both behaviors

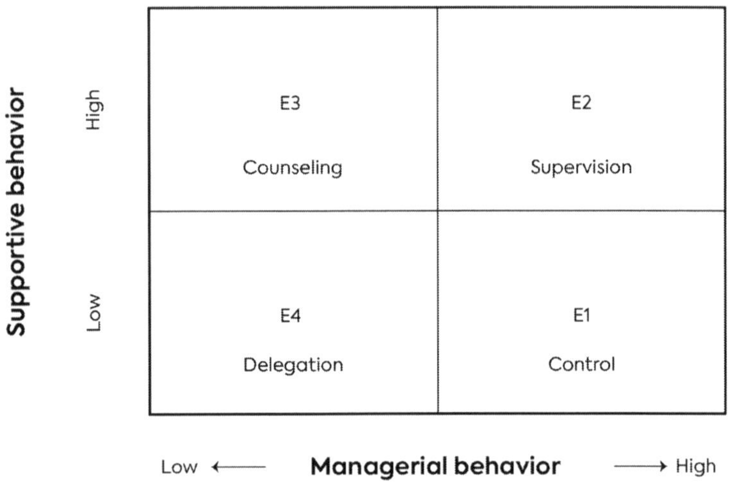

Source: XXI Century Marketing[4]

On the other hand, these situational leadership styles fit seamlessly into the four levels of team development in which the leader:

Level 1: Controls

Level 2: Supervises

Level 3: Advises

Level 4: Delegates

4 González, R. (2014). Marketing en el siglo XXI. DEF. Marketing XXI.

Tools of Today's Leader

I have mentioned some tools or qualities that a leader must have; however, I will be more specific here. A leader must:

- Communicate in an assertive manner
- Be able to promote an inclusive culture regardless of age, race, ethnicity, gender, ability status, national origin, gender identity
- Recognize the different attitudes, priorities, styles, talents, and values of their collaborators
- Be respectful, open, and friendly
- Collaborate with people from other generations
- Value and recognize opportunities for partnership and contribution
- Demonstrate a willingness to share resources and learning
- Promote an intergenerational learning environment through training programs
- Understand and identify where they are and where they want to go
- Be emotionally intelligent

Leadership is not about being in charge; it's about taking care of the people in our charge.
Simon Sinek

Leadership has gone through different eras and points of view, as we have already seen, leading to today's leadership approaches. As stated in the introduction, the approach proposed in this book is directly relates to EI and SI. So, in the next chapter, we will explore EI and SI in depth. But before we get to these concepts, below you will find some vital points to refresh the knowledge acquired in this chapter and some exercises that will be very useful for your process. See you in the next chapter!

Bullet points

- The leader is born and made; leadership is a learning process.
- Learn to live with four generations in the same work environment.
- There is a differentiation between the leader and the manager: the former innovates and the latter only manages.
- In today's era, it is necessary in order to evolve to break away from the system that forces everyone to think and act in the same way.
- Situational leadership perfectly adjusts to the particular situation the leader faces.
- Intergenerational leadership seeks to establish agreements between leaders belonging to different generations.
- When the leader makes a change, they acquire knowledge and innovative tools to address clear objectives.

Suggested Exercise

After learning about the different approaches, styles, competencies, and characteristics of leadership, it is time to evaluate yourself and determine your leadership style at this moment. Remember, there is no one right leadership style. You can work to adapt to a different, more appealing leadership style.

1. Which leadership style(s) do you identify with? Why?

____

____

____

____

____

____

2. Now that you have identified which style or styles you identify with, it is time to review your style(s) through the following format:

Elements and tools	
I have	
I lack	
I must integrate	
I must adjust	

Source: Bárbara Flores Caballero

Keywords

Leadership · Eras of Leadership · Situational Leadership · Intergenerational Leadership · Fourth Industrial Revolution · Organizations · Generation X · Generation Y · Generation Z · Diversity · Leadership Styles · Baby Boomers · Millennial · Centennial · Organizational Leadership · Impact · Purpose · Integrity · Commitment · Inspire · Influence · Respect · Emotional Intelligence

Sources of Information

Bass, M. (1990). *Theory, research, and managerial applications*. The Free Press.

Burns, J. (1978). *Leadership*. Harper & Row.

Chiles, S., Valentino, C. y Hattam, J. (s. f.). *Caja de herramientas de liderazgo intergeneracional para la conservación: aumentar nuestro alcance* [Intergenerational leadership toolkit for conservation): growing our reach. GrowingOurReach. https://repository.netecweb.org/exhibits/show/leadership-esp

Conexión Esan. (January 21, 2011). *El líder nace y se hace* [Leaders are born and made]. Esan. https://www.esan.edu.pe/conexion-esan/el-lider-nace-y-se-hace

Díaz Chica, O. (2018). *Avances en liderazgo: el modelo situacional.* [Advancements in Leadership: The Situational Model]. Editorial Technos.

Robbins, S. (2009). *Comportamiento organizacional* [Organizational behavior]. *(13.a ed.).* Pearson Prentice Hall.

CHAPTER 2:

LEADING WITH THE HEART

People with well-developed emotional skills are also more likely to be content and efficient in life, mastering the habits of the mind that foster their own productivity.

Daniel Goleman

Who Decides?[5]

Two friends met for breakfast, but first one of them stopped by the newsstand to buy a newspaper. Upon doing so, he greeted the vendor politely. The vendor, on the other hand, responded rudely and threw the newspaper at him in an inconsiderate and rude manner. On the contrary, the buyer smiled kindly and in a leisurely fashion wished him a good day and thanked him for his service.

The two friends continued their way and when they were sufficiently away from the newsstand, the other said to him:

"Hey, does this man always treat you like this?"

"Yes, every day," said the friend.

"And you are always so polite and kind to him?"

"Yes, I am."

"Could you explain to me why you are so nice to him, if he is so unkind to you?"

The friend answered:

"It is very easy. I don't want him to be the one to decide how I behave."

To be emotionally intelligent is to be responsible for your emotions and reactions, but not for the emotions and reactions of others.

Bárbara Flores Caballero

---

5 Scharrenberg, J. (2017). *Quien te enfada te controla* [Who makes you angry controls you]. Sloyu Mindfulness.

If I were to ask you with which of these two friends' reactions you identify with, what would you answer? In fact, the most important thing is that both reactions are linked to our thoughts and emotions, to the way we relate and act. Most important, this is also a choice. Actually, it is possible to learn how to behave, taking into account the management of our thoughts and emotions within any environment, including an organizational one. In fact, this is a key factor in exercising optimal leadership.

Nowadays, it is common to hear the term EI beyond academic spaces or the universe of psychology, so much so that organizations have also been increasing their implementation of EI within the different areas that comprise them. This concept is directly related to the two friends in the story at the beginning of this chapter and is another clear piece of evidence that the evolution of the business world is a reality.

Nowadays, organizations are looking for professionals with specific skills that include the identification and management of emotions, something that applies to both leaders and collaborators. They are looking for people like the friend who did not allow the newsstand attendant to decide his behavior or conditions in which he would behave, which could be applied not only to people but also to situations.

This is where EI comes into play, with the goal of achieving optimal performance in all aspects. That is how important it is to understand the details of this concept from an organizational perspective. Therefore, I want to dedicate this chapter to EI.

Getting to Know Emotional Intelligence

Although you probably have a notion of the concept of EI, I would like to start by accurately defining what it consists of. Simply put, EI is about identifying and managing one's own emotions and those of others. Of course, this is not something improvised; in fact, there are many theorists who offer their own conceptualization of what EI is.

Wayne Payne is widely credited with the first use of the term EI, specifically cited in his 1985 doctoral thesis titled *A Study of Emotions*. However, this term had already been coined in 1966 in texts by Leuner (Bar-On, 2000). Notwithstanding, this idea was not mature compared to the EI we use today in a clearer and more complete way.

Before Payne wrote his thesis, Howard Gardner in 1983 put forth his theory of multiple intelligences, a much more comprehensive position. He identified a) interpersonal intelligence, the ability to understand other people's motivations, intentions, and desires; and b) intrapersonal intelligence, which consists of understanding oneself, meaning, appreciating our feelings, including fears and motivations. Something very important about these concepts is that in both cases we are dealing with capabilities. Why is this so important? Because since they are capabilities, it is possible to develop them. In addition, for Gardner (1999), intelligence indicators such as IQ, do not explain in depth the cognitive capacity of human beings; we not only acquire theoretical knowledge, but we also manage feelings that produce different emotions.

It is very important to understand that emotional intelligence is not the opposite of intelligence, it is not the triumph of the heart over the head, it is the intersection of both.
David Caruso

Stanley Greenspan presented a model in 1989, but it was not published until 1995 when the Daniel Goleman's famous book *Emotional Intelligence* led to numerous publications dealing with EI in the sense that we use it today. Goleman was one of the pioneers in naming another type of intelligence and he was the one who really popularized this notion.

Goleman (1996) defines EI as "the ability to perceive and express emotions, to assimilate emotions into thought, to understand and reason with emotions, and to regulate emotions in oneself and others." This is the definition for which my proposal fits best.

Having reached this point, I would like to clarify the concept of EI. Following Goleman's definition, let's look at it using an example. If we review and analyze the word "worker" in labor terms, it seems to mean something difficult, a concept that involves effort which is heavy. Nowadays, we talk about the collaborator because, precisely, that is what the person does, collaborates in the organization and implements actions in an efficient manner; it is necessary to manage from a collaborative sense. This change represents a different perception, a person will feel differently when being called a collaborator or a leader; additionally, in the organization, EI is being introduced in an adequate way, with leaders thus showing a real understanding of the members of their team.

As we can see, EI represents a total paradigm shift, considering what we now have at our disposal a knowledge that allows us to recognize and understand that the mind, many times, can be subjected to limiting beliefs or the memory of unexpected consequences resulting from previous experiences. Thus, we must ask, "What is the ideal way to manage our emotions when faced with difficult situations?"

When awareness is brought to an emotion,
power is brought to your life.
Tara Meyer-Robson

Understanding that we now have this knowledge, we are in an era today where we can develop our leadership aspects; we have reached a higher level of awareness and intuition. It is not only about looking with our eyes, but with all the senses; in this way it is possible to identify how the other feels. Also, we must listen to what a person says, in what tone they say it, how they say it and observing or being attentive to their body language, because not only the words, but the whole body is talking about how they feel. And from that place we must be attentive.

As has become clear, there are many factors and aspects involved in the concept of leadership. Therefore, it is necessary to deepen in all the tools that are at your disposal to achieve optimal performance as a leader, EI being one of your greatest allies to achieve your proposed objectives.

Emotional Intelligence and Leadership, Inseparable Allies

A person who is at a high level of leadership is more exposed to the opinion of his collaborators and other leaders, from both the point of view of his performance and of other more personal aspects. So it is essential that the person also develops their EI. While I agree with the authors cited in reviewing a bit of the history and the concept itself, it is important that you can increase your own EI. Let's get to it!

Developing stronger emotional intelligence is one of the biggest challenges that leaders face at all levels of organizations.
Stephen Covey

At this point, I would like to share with you a very revealing experience that registered a very interesting and enriching outcome. At the age of 33, I was appointed Vice President of Planning and Development at an educational institution in Puerto Rico. On my team was a man who was already in his sixties, something that caught my attention. Of course, I wanted to talk to him, his experience had to be remarkable and therefore very valuable.

In doing so, he told me that he had been in every position, even the highest ones, but now I was going to be his boss, something that did not seem to please him. Then he said, "I want to tell you that I don't want to work with you, you are younger than me and I have more experience. I will continue in my office, although I want you to know that I will do the minimum. When I feel ready, if that happens, then I will let you know."

At that time, I was finishing my EdD that would make me an expert in EI; still, I wondered how I would handle that situation, since I had to deal with it and I understood it as an emergency. Obviously, I had been working and researching EI in depth, so I appealed to it. I understood that he felt threatened, so I decided to be compassionate and give him space, as well as to be empathetic and put myself in his shoes.

The next few days, I greeted him with respect and maintained a good attitude, even putting on music. After about a month, it was clear he had started to feel that good energy. The next step was to start incorporating him in all my work. To get him to integrate, I told him, "I talked to the president in a meeting, and you have to be next to me, shoulder to shoulder, you are a person who has a lot of knowledge." That is how I started including him in everything.

One day he came up to me and commented, “I want you to know that I respect you very much, that I am your ally. I am not going to leave you. I am getting onboard, and we are going to row the ship together. I admire you greatly, because at your young age your EI is extremely high.” When I left my position, because I had to move, he had prepared a poem for me together with my assistant, and even let out a few tears. We still maintain our friendship via social networks.

With this experience I can prove that, thanks to being compassionate and going through all those phases of empathy, I was able to have this sixty-something year-old colleague on my side. Both compassion and empathy are key elements for EI, as well as good communication that builds trust.

If we refer to this example, it is possible to note that not only a healthy and compassionate bond was established, projected from EI, but it went further, creating an emotional and spiritual connection. It was possible to take this gentleman to a level of understanding that had no return and he was never the same again, something that I was able to confirm later.

Emotional intelligence is the ability to sense, understand and effectively apply the power and acumen of emotions as a source of human energy, information, confidence, creativity, and influence.
Robert Cooper

For a leader it is not only about practicing active listening, which is fundamental, but it goes beyond that to establishing a genuine connection with collaborators. It is about being attentive to body language, to every detail. The EI leader will be able to read what a person is feeling; therefore, they must be able to observe, listen, connect, and communicate.

In addition, by being aware, a leader can constantly work on enhancing the tools related to EI and to improve their own performance and that of their collaborators. On the other hand, connecting with collaborators must also address the diversity of the team and their individual strengths to engage them in a positive way. Let's not forget that we are emotional and social beings, and we must focus this vision of leadership from that premise. In addition, a leader must see the glass as full, that is to say, privilege positive thoughts because it also inspires others. The leader must be able to generate positive situations if they want to obtain positive results. The ideal is to evaluate collaborators to measure their level of EI before establishing strategies from this perspective.

Krén and Séllei (2020), in their research titled *The Role of Emotional Intelligence in Organizational Performanc*, argue the following:

> Leaders are the main figures in organizations. Their emotionally intelligent behavior is critical from the point of view of organizational effectiveness. That is why their level of emotional intelligence and their emotionally intelligent behavior need to be examined.

At the end of this chapter, you will find a short, very simple EI self-assessment that will give you an idea of how you are doing in this regard. However, it is necessary to take into account the importance of investing in this aspect not only for the leader, but also for human resources (HR) departments.

An empowered organization is one in which individuals have the knowledge, skill, desire, and opportunity to personally succeed in a way that leads to collective organizational success.
Stephen Covey

It is entirely possible to train in this sense, since the results of a more specialized test are not enough. EI must be monitored and become part of the organizational climate, including comparing the results obtained by the organization in a given period. However, it should be clear that a difference will be made if real training and prevention strategies for EI are established.

We must not forget that EI is the basis of the leadership management model that I propose, an approach that pursues labor efficiency, savings, and profitability for organizations.

The Partners of Emotional Intelligence

I have already mentioned, even exemplified, some of the elements present in everything involved in the EI approach; however, it is time to explain these elements in greater detail: self-knowledge, self-regulation, motivation, empathy, and social skills.

1. Self-Knowledge

This element has been very important since ancient times. Even the Greek philosopher Aristotle noted, "To know oneself is the beginning of all wisdom." This is not a coincidence. From the proposed approach it is possible to say that it is characterized by knowing how to set healthy limits, that is to say, also knowing how to say no.

When a leader has self-confidence, they are able to set limits, which is vital. As a leader, it is about knowing what you need, being true to yourself and taking care of yourself first in order to be able to work with your collaborators. It is important to know and be aware of how and why you feel in a particular way, but from your own standards, which are not absolute but nevertheless valid.

Experimenting with your own emotions and feelings in a conscious manner —that is, gaining self-knowledge—is an integral part of learning.
Joshua Freedman

Today's leader must be self-aware from the perspective of knowing what their strengths and those of others are. In addition, it is important to be able to see what as a leader you can learn from others. On the other hand, this leader must not worry, but get busy in order to project to others about what can be provided. This leader is also clear about how far they want to go and how far they want to allow others to go.

Suggested Exercise

Below you will find a SWOT exercise (strengths, weaknesses, opportunities, and threats). I have designed this tool especially for you, in order to analyze your leadership skills and to get to know yourself as a great ally for self-knowledge. You only have to answer the questions posed and analyze them in a very honest manner, this will help you to know yourself better as a leader.

Strengths

1. What resources do you have?

____

____

2. What is your knowledge with respect to your role as a leader?

____

____

3. What are your experiences as a leader and how can they help you?

4. What are your skills and capabilities?

5. What are your talents?

Opportunities

1. What prevents you from achieving your goals?

2. What resources and information do you need?

3. What knowledge do you need?

4. What skills do you need to acquire to achieve your goals?

5. What do you gain if you achieve your goal?

Weaknesses

1. What are the limitations that prevent you from achieving your objectives?

2. What are your fears?

3. What keeps you from moving forward?

4. What are your limiting thoughts?

5. What type of training do you think you need to strengthen your skills or acquire new skills?

Threats

1. What external factors could prevent you from achieving your goals?

____

____

2. What external limitations will you encounter along the way?

____

____

3. What situation might you be afraid of?

4. What elements could appear in your path that could prevent you from moving forward?

5. What national or international context could be negative?

Source: Bárbara Flores Caballero

2. Self-Regulation

This aspect has to do with the consciousness of the leader in the here and now, their inner look. Being in the now is a major factor, because it is necessary to take that space for oneself. Self-regulation is related to emotions; that is precisely what we want to regulate. In the same way, leader seeks to do this with their collaborators, wanting to guide them so that they can develop this capacity.

You can't always control the wind,
but you can control your sails.
Bob Chope

Suppose we have to go into a meeting and some small event that we consider negative has altered the course of our daily routine. We can change our focus at that moment and think of something pleasant; for example, evoking an unforgettable trip or calling someone and talking about something else. This is self-regulation: disconnecting from a thought that has taken us out of context and being able to focus on the now without being tied to the emotion that has produced the dysregulation.

It is necessary to connect with positive emotions to be able to self-regulate. Now, in today's leadership, self-regulation also includes showing ourselves to be more human. So, it is very important to analyze that which affects us, and to eliminate that information that is not useful and does not serve us. It is an internal work, but not merely self-control, which has to do with the external and how we handle ourselves with others. Although this is also important, it is necessary to differentiate them.

Emotional self-regulation is the result of hard work, not an inherent skill.
Travis Bradberry

Suggested Exercise

To achieve efficient self-regulation, Edmund Jacobson's (1987) progressive relaxation is a physiological method that leads to deep relaxation, which can reduce stress (Payne, 2005). Below, you will find a series distributed in three phases comprised of simple steps to achieve relaxation. Do not forget to follow the order presented.

Phase 1. Tension-Relaxation:

- Relaxation of the face, neck, and shoulders.
- Forehead: Contract your forehead for a few seconds and relax slowly.
- Eyes: Open your eyes wide and then close them very slowly.
- Nose: Contract your nose for a few seconds, then relax slowly.
- Mouth: Smile widely, relax slowly.
- Tongue: Press your tongue against the roof of your mouth, now relax slowly.
- Jaw: With your lips closed, bite down with some intensity, notice the tension in the lateral muscles of your face and temples, now relax slowly.
- Lips: Pucker them as if you were going to give a kiss, after a few seconds, relax slowly.
- Neck and nape of neck: Bend your neck backwards for a few seconds, return to the starting

position; now do the same forward, and return to the starting position slowly.

- Shoulders and neck: Raise your shoulders by pressing them against the neck, after a few seconds, slowly return to the starting position.
- Relaxation of arms and hands: Contract, without moving it, first one arm and then the other with a clenched fist, notice the tension in your arms, forearms, and hands. Now relax slowly.
- Leg relaxation: First stretch one leg and then the other, lifting the foot up and feeling the tension in each leg, buttock, thigh, knee, calf, and foot. Then slowly relax.
- Relaxation of the thorax, abdomen, and lumbar region.
- Sit in a chair and relax.
- Back: Place your arms in a cross position and bring your elbows back. Notice the tension in your lower back and shoulders.
- Thorax: Inhale and hold the air for a few seconds in your lungs. Notice the tension in your chest. Now exhale slowly.
- Stomach: Contract your stomach for a few seconds, then slowly relax it.

- Waist: Contract your buttocks and thighs, noticing how you rise a little in the chair.

Phase 2. Review: Mentally review each of the parts you have tensed and relaxed, checking that each remains relaxed. Now relax each one even more.

Phase 3. Mental relaxation: Finally think of something pleasant for you that relaxes you, maybe some kind of music, a landscape, or a memory. You can also leave your mind blank.

This practice helps us to connect with our body and emotions in the three phases mentioned above, with a duration between ten and fifteen minutes, without carrying it out in a rushed manner. Do not forget that you can use this technique several times a day.

3. Motivation

This is a vital element for every human being; it can become the engine that drives us to achieve the goals we have set. From the ideal vision proposed by a leader, it is necessary to mention that there are two types of motivation: intrinsic motivation and extrinsic motivation. Let us imagine that we sit on a swing, and someone pushes us, but then we keep ourselves on our own in that swing, even controlling the power and speed. The hand that pushes us, for example, an external factor, would be the extrinsic motivation. The fact of keeping moving would be the intrinsic one, what internally keeps us motivated. At this point the question would be: What drives us?

When talking about intrinsic motivation, we must ask ourselves: What is it that drives us and comes from within ourselves? We must explore ourselves internally and learn, to have rewards, for example, based on what brings us happiness or pleasure. This is what motivates us. By having high motivation, we are able to achieve our goals. Intrinsic motivation involves a share of responsibility of each team member, not only of the leader, but also of the collaborators.

Extrinsic motivation originates outside of us, for example, when we are awarded a prize or offered a promotion. Moreover, it involves social acceptance. But, who accepts us extrinsically? That is the question.

People need a purpose that has meaning,
but with a shared purpose,
we are capable of achieving anything.
Warren Bennis

Motivation is aligned with purpose. In the case of what I propose, it is necessary that the person's purpose is also aligned with that of the organization. Why? Because the achievement of objectives is directly related to both elements, if everything operates properly as a single big gear, the results will be positive.

If we question ourselves about what motivates us, there are many possible answers, it could be achievement, affiliation, or positioning, even all three. For example, impacting our collaborators or achieving positive results is achievement-driven motivation. This not only motivates the leader, but the whole team, and this is really key. In addition, incentives are an important source of motivation; for example, earning more money or traveling.

For all this and more, it is vital to understand what drives people, but how do you know? A good tool to obtain this valuable information is a 100% confidential survey, a simple and very effective method that allows us to better understand, from this perspective, leaders and collaborators.

Another way to obtain information about what motivates people is to resort to what the psychologist Abraham Maslow proposed in his theory on motivation. In it, he explains precisely what drives human behavior.

Why is this important to our approach? Because for a collaborator "the path begins when the need of the lower order (i.e., physiology and security) is covered" (Perez, 2020).

If we apply Maslow's hierarchy of needs this means that in addition to receiving remuneration for their services, this being one of their initial motivations for being part of an organization we must not forget that the first concern of the collaborator is to cover their basic needs. In addition, we would be talking about, for example, having adequate space to be able to perform work functions in a pleasant environment. Once these needs are met, there will be a settling-in stage that includes other benefits.

Of course, when true motivation is achieved, the needs of affiliation come into play, so interpersonal relationships play a fundamental role. When the organization enhances this cooperation among collaborators, it obtains better performance by creating an appropriate work environment. If this organization wishes to generate a genuine feeling of belonging, it must make each collaborator feel that they are taken into account. Then, the team will develop new motivations.

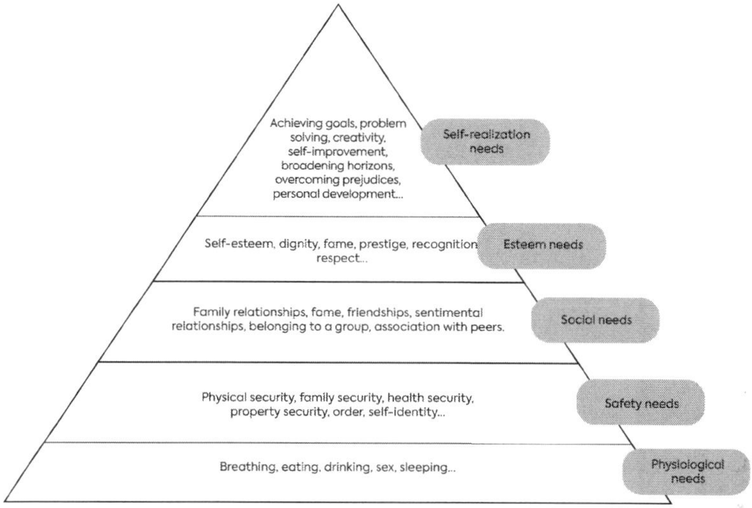

Source: A Theory of Human Motivation (Maslow, 2013).

A leader must be self-motivated, be able to manage themselves, carry out creative activities, strengthen self-confidence and encourage their collaborators to do the same. We must not lose sight of the fact that they need to have a motivated team to achieve goals as a group, but also individually. The leader wants to increase the team's energy and knows that they can achieve this by self-motivation; for example, by eating or sleeping properly, reading a book, getting up early, or meditating. In addition, it is necessary to establish good communication, something the leader achieves from a positive or optimistic approach.

It is necessary for a leader to monitor their progress and set new goals, but also understand that if the leader does not know themself, it will be very difficult to motivate self or others every day and in a permanent manner. I invite you, as a leader, to motivate your team by using your EI. To do this, you can use various simple techniques or strategies with your team members. For example: provide feedback, offer professional development options, maintain constant and active communication, promote a collaborative work environment, celebrate achievements, recognize successful work individually and collectively, show interest in your employees' problems, and be flexible, among others.

Something that should not be overlooked is generational motivation; for example, baby boomers like to be recognized extrinsically, but generation Z works more from motivation. Without motivation it is not possible to integrate or get results.

In fact, a Randstad study titled Employer Branding. When Perception Can Become Reality (Pérez, 2020) points out that gender, age, and level of education are also key factors that generate variations in the order of priority of the needs proposed by Maslow.

In view of the above, and considering the age factor, establishing a system of needs could contribute to a better organization to achieve your objectives. A true leader takes into account every detail of this aspect, observes the motivation of themself and their collaborators in an integral manner.

Suggested Exercise

I would like to share with you a dynamic of questions that I ask you to answer with the utmost sincerity.

1. Think of a wish that has been fulfilled. Now ask yourself: How did you achieve it, how did you feel, why did you do it or what was your motivation?

   ____

   ____

2. Try to think of a wish that has not yet been fulfilled, but that you hope will be fulfilled in the future. Now think: What can you do, what motivates you to achieve it, how can you achieve it, how would you feel, why are you going to try, for what reasons are you going to achieve it?

   ____

   ____

3. Now imagine something that you don't like, but that you must do. Answer yourself: What is your attitude towards it, what do you do in terms of that obligation, how do you feel, how will you do it, why will you do it?

4. Faced with what you dislike and have thought about in the previous question, go back to the first point of the dynamic and motivate yourself by thinking about what you are capable of achieving. Write a mantra to motivate yourself.

Source: Bárbara Flores Caballero

4. Empathy

The first thing I would like to make clear is that I understand empathy as "the attitude that a person has to recognize the emotions of others. That is to say, it is the ability to understand the feelings of others and to be able to read their nonverbal messages" (Goleman, 1996). In plain words, it means putting oneself in the other person's shoes. However, this is not a unique concept. Psychologists Daniel Goleman and Paul Ekman acknowledge three types of empathy (Goleman and Ekman, 2017):

- Cognitive: Understanding what you think as a leader and understanding what the other is experiencing; it means that you can establish effective communication with your collaborator(s).
- Emotional: Understanding how the other person feels and, starting from this, building a connection with this person.
- Compassionate: Going beyond, helping where you can, asking questions or taking the initiative to help the other, offering alternatives.

In addition, active listening is a great ally of empathy; for example, not interrupting the other person when they are talking or looking at the phone without paying attention but, on the contrary, maintaining eye contact. In addition, it is about not judging or assuming, being able to understand when a person just needs to be heard and when they require your advice and recommendations because of your leadership role. Being empathetic means being compassionate and understanding, not complacent.

When you show deep empathy towards others, your defensive energy goes down and positive energy replaces it. That is when you can get more creative in solving problems.
Stephen Covey

Suggested Exercise

In this exercise you must literally put yourself in the other person's shoes:

1. Think of a person you know who, for some reason, you don't feel comfortable around. Write down their name.

   ____

   ____

2. Analyze: What is it specifically that you don't like about that person?

   ____

   ____

3. Remember their home or office, remember the details of their environment and their life, even their family, as much as you know, as much as you can.

4. Now put yourself in their place, visualize yourself in their clothes and shoes, in their environment and imagine as realistically as possible something that person should do; think how and why they do it.

5. Stay as long as you can in their shoes imagining different situations and trying to solve them with the resources that person has.

6. After that experience, go back to your shoes and analyze it well. Think: do you feel the same way about that person as you did before?

Source: Bárbara Flores Caballero

5. Social Skills

It is necessary for a leader to have the ability to train their collaborators and future leaders. In addition, they must be able to integrate their team around an idea in order to work together and obtain the desired results.

Upon any idea proposed by one of their collaborators, it is necessary for the leader to apply active listening and then ask, why, what for, and how? By allowing collaborators to express their ideas, a desirable climate of trust will be generated. It is not a matter of rejecting ideas, but of deepening the idea according to the impact on the organization. It is important that leaders offer a humane, motivating, exemplifying, and inspiring response so as not to prevent other ideas from coming in.

Find your voice and inspire others to find theirs.
Stephen Covey

It is necessary for the leader to encourage team cooperation, conflict resolution, decision making, problem solving, collaboration and bond building. On the other hand, the leader must not forget effective communication and the influence they can exert. In addition, the leader must establish a collaborative networking, internal and external, as an asset that generates a return on investment in which all parties win.

One of the ways to capitalize on social skills with your work team, or even with the people around you, is to use a tone of voice that matches their facial expressions in a friendly manner. Also, coordinate your body movements according to the message you wish to express. This will help reinforce the message and project greater credibility.

The Five Factors of Emotional Intelligence

A leader must go beyond, connecting thoughts, emotions, and behaviors; therefore, it is necessary to:

1. Identify thoughts
2. Manage thoughts, since they come before emotions
3. Know how to identify emotions
4. Manage emotions
5. Watch over conduct and behavior

Recommendation: This small but very valuable list could be used by leaders to manage your day-to-day life as they face the situations that arise.

Situations that Demonstrate the Impact of Emotional Intelligence in Organizations

As we all know, in the year 2020, the world's population was faced with a great challenge: the pandemic. We were all confined to our homes in the midst of a completely unknown context that affected us all. Faced with this extreme situation, how did EI make an influence?

A team made up of researchers from different Peruvian universities proposed an investigation that sought to answer this question; they published a report titled *Influence of*

Emotional Intelligence on the Institutional Climate in Regular Basic Education teachers in Times of Pandemic (Menacho-Vargas et al., 2022). The first step consisted of surveying 139 teachers in an educational institution through a questionnaire consisting of 43 items that considered the following dimensions: self-knowledge, self-regulation, motivation, empathy, and social skills. Once the results were analyzed, these researchers demonstrated that 25.5% of the variability of the institutional climate was related to EI and its dimensions.

Researchers at University Tun Hussein Onn of Malaysia did the same, albeit in a business context, published in a report titled *The Influence of Emotional Intelligence and Coping Strategies on Employee Productivity Performance During COVID-19 Pandemic* (Lim & Hamid, 2021). After surveying 50 members of the organization using a twelve-question survey, it was concluded that, indeed, EI influenced the productivity and performance of collaborators. In this case, it obtained a positive correlation coefficient of 0.661 (920).

In fact, the Malaysian researchers went further, recommending that organizations should acknowledge this fact and implement training plans with regard to improving emotional capabilities. And this is exactly what I recommend to all organizations, since not only will they obtain greater productivity, but their organizational climate and profitability will be impacted in a very positive way. Are you still wondering if it is really necessary to develop your EI?

Emotional Intelligence vs. Intellectual Intelligence

After understanding what EI consists of, we can see that it is not defined by intellectual intelligence. In fact, Goleman (1998) pointed out that some professors (i.e., Martin Seligman, University of Pennsylvania; Walter Mischel, Stanford University; and Peter Salovey, Yale University) admitted that IQ accounted for only 20% of the factors that determine success, with the remaining 80% linked to other factors that include what they called EI.

So how do we achieve a balance between the two? That is the question we must analyze. The answer will reveal the necessary keys.

Intellectual intelligence is related to IQ and to a person's skills from a technical point of view. Undoubtedly, it has to do with various skills that human beings have, such as memory, attention, perception, and lexicon, among others.

The real challenge is to show that emotional intelligence matters over and above psychological constructs that have been measured for decades, like personality or IQ.

Peter Salovey

In saying this, I am not referring to a confrontation between these two types of intelligence, but to finding the right balance between them. This will depend on the different situations and decisions we have to face. From the perspective of this book, it is more important to cultivate EI, of course, without abandoning the intellectual. Of course, today EI is much more highly valued than before.

Then, we must ask ourselves, who wins between the two? The answer is that there need not be such a duel, since there can exist an adapted balance, as long as we approach it from compassion and commitment. Examples such as Steve Jobs and Bill Gates show that intellectual intelligence alone is not enough.

In some interviews I have had the opportunity to hear leaders say that they have achieved something, wherein they are always the protagonists, they speak from the "I." This sets off red flags, because they are not taking into consideration their team. In addition, when asked about the most difficult thing they had to face, they often mention something that does not seem to be a real challenge.

It is also possible to find others who show a high level of EI, but do not have a sense of belonging in the organization. This could be a consequence of not belonging to the team of a true leader; rather they may have worked under the mandate of a boss. Nowadays we are looking for leaders not bosses.

It is urgent for organizations to evaluate and identify whether the professionals who have personnel under their charge exercise the role of a boss or a true leader. Once identified, action must be promoted in order to achieve significant change.

Goleman conducted a study in which he gathered information from specialists in training and HR development for his competency model which he derived from 181 types of jobs in 121 companies around the world. Once he was able to separate technical competencies from emotions, to later compare their relative importance, he found that three skills considered vital for success were emotional competencies—integrity, adaptability, and talent for collaboration.

These findings were supported by more in-depth studies that have shown that emotional competencies are now twice as important for people to succeed, beyond possessing intelligence or technical knowledge. This is why more and more companies are modifying the way they train and promote their people (Fisher, 2002).

How to Develop the Emotional Intelligence of a Leader

Each of us is capable of learning from experiences, both positive and negative, but the decision to take on this learning is completely personal and there is a high probability that it will not be repeated. If a leader decides to learn from all experiences, even if they perceive them firsthand as a negative experience, then they will become positive experiences.

Emotional education is the ability to listen to almost anything without losing your temper or your self-confidence.

Robert Frost

When talking about the leader, in this sense, the first thing a leader must do to develop the capacity for EI is to connect with themself. How? By engaging in introspection that allows the leader to obtain information about themself and to be able to develop their EI in an optimal manner.

This introspection can be done by asking questions and answering them honestly. For example: Who am I really? What are my interests? What worries me about the future? What is the most important thing in my life? What do I need to change about myself?

In addition to these personal questions, leaders must also focus on their role as a leader. Do I give clear instructions? Do I give timely feedback? Do I give credit to those who do the work? Am I available to my team? Do I get angry when plans are not followed? Am I respectful? Do I provide opportunities for growth? And so on.

Then, once a leader identifies that their internal assessment is okay, they should continue to work but look outward. How? By checking on the status of their empathy or social skills. In addition, it is important to look at other people, because you can also learn from them, as well as listening in every way, always from a positive perspective. It could even be very valuable to ask collaborators for help, acknowledging their skills and talents in a genuine manner. Moreover, a leader can develop their EI from their own experience. How? By reviewing their thoughts and emotions in the face of different situations. If reacting by feeling anger, is it because the cerebral amygdala has been activated, and this is related to traumas or difficult experiences. In that case, it is necessary to discover why the leader feels the way they feel, to heal that part of their life in order to move forward.

Seek first to understand, then be understood.
Stephen Covey

From this understanding, the leader must practice solidarity, especially in situations considered conflictive, but it is necessary to do it from a broad perspective of alternatives. It is also very important to discard words such as "problem" for something that is simply a situation.

This change in the code of language is vital because words are capable of creating reality. According to Robert Dilts (2003), the influence of language makes it possible to deactivate limiting mental models and replace them with others that are beneficial. It is advisable for the leader to reprogram their linguistic code in this sense and take into account that language, the spoken word in particular, is also about how tone as well actions are carried out.

By simply changing words to more positive ones, this reprogramming will be noticeable. Also, the leader must not forget the importance of communication characterized as being assertive; the fact of managing this change in code will enrich the power of communication. On the other hand, it is not advisable to overlook the cultural diversity within an organization; simply put, it is not the same to talk to a person of Honduran heritage as it is to talk to a person of Japanese heritage. They are completely different cultures; therefore, it is advisable to know a little more about culture to understand and connect more easily.

Thus, it may be desirable that HR departments provide voluntary information about the origin of the collaborators, this would allow for better understanding and, therefore, the development of deeper EI from an empathic point of view. Leaders must create an organizational climate for their team to foster EI without forgetting the importance of a high level of respect. People are meant to be seen as a whole and not mere individual beings. Relationships are also built from this outlook. A leader can teach their collaborators through emotions.

Social Intelligence

Although in this chapter we have been discussing everything related to EI —a field in which I have been trained—from an organizational perspective it is also essential that we do not ignore the fact that we are gregarious beings. We necessarily relate in different ways with other people and we establish partnerships that we adjust for different purposes; for example, between the leader and their team of collaborators.

For this reason, at this point, I will be supported by Saraí González Berríos, expert in the area of HR and founder of the HR and supervision consulting firm Assertive Connections, who has very important contributions for the leadership approach I am proposing.

Understanding Social Intelligence

The concept of SI has emerged as a new paradigm when we think about how we interact with others. SI facilitates the understanding of people's thoughts and actions that make up our environments. But, what exactly is SI?

In 1920 the American psychologist Edward Thorndike began to refer to this concept of SI (Essex, 2018) interpreting it as the ability to understand others, knowing how to deal with them and behave wisely in relationships, dealing with an intelligence that considers cognitive and behavioral elements. Goleman (2006) defined SI as a skill that allows us to capture practically instantaneously the mood of other people, their feelings, motivations and fears, and interact with them effectively. According to Goleman, SI comes into play whenever there is an encounter between two or more people.

The art of communication is the language of leadership.
James Humes

Goleman divides SI into two subcategories or competencies. First are personal competencies, the ability to grasp the different aspects of one's own emotional life. Second are social competencies, the way in which we understand others and relate to them.

Components of Social Intelligence

Goleman acknowledges two major categories that characterize SI.

1. First is social consciousness, what we feel about other people. Social consciousness is divided into four elements:
    - Primordial Empathy: This consists of feeling the feelings of others and correctly interpreting those emotional signs that are not verbal; this is related to intuitive and visceral skills that are activated, practically and automatically.
    - Attunement: This is about connecting with others and listening to them in a genuinely receptive way, allowing us to be fully aware of the way others speak, establishing dialogues.
    - Empathic Accuracy: This requires primordial empathy and is the most notable skill of SI, the ability to understand feelings, emotions, and intentions of others.
    - Social Cognition: This is the ability to understand how the social world works. Therefore, it is about knowing how to behave with probity. In addition, this skill allows decoding signs and signals in social environments.

2. Second is social competence, what we do with our social awareness. This has four components:

- Synchrony: This component is the basis for the other social skills because it consists of possessing the ease to relate to others on a non-verbal level.
- Self-presentation: This consists of projecting an adequate image of oneself, requiring a special charisma that allows the awakening of emotions in others that they themselves experience.
- Influence: This is about taking advantage of the different social interactions, modeling them in the correct way.
- Interest in others: This consists not only of showing interest and concern for other people, but also in acting in a congruent manner.

Social Brain

Since I have already mentioned the brain, it is time to define the brain's social component, which is, in fact, a set of neural mechanisms that guide the process of our relationships; therefore, it possesses a sum of thoughts, memories, feelings and emotions related to our social interactions.

Also, it involves interpersonal skills, such as empathy and interest that surpasses our search for personal good. A leader with a high level of SI takes others into account and enriches their interpersonal relationships.

On the other hand, it is important for you to know that social skills are produced through mirror neurons, which allow us to recognize the emotions in others and identify with the message or element that they transmit to us. In addition, they are also largely responsible for the phenomenon of emotional contagion, considering that they help us to understand what is happening, to be empathetic and to connect with others.

Empathy represents the foundational skill for all the social competencies important for work.
Daniel Goleman

Empathy, the Secret Weapon of Social Intelligence

Now, as has already been made clear, empathy is an essential connector between people, but at this point I would like to emphasize that through it we can recognize emotions in others and, therefore, the process of understanding is facilitated. I would like to share with you five recommendations, suggested by Saraí to promote empathy through verbal and non-verbal channels:

- Establish eye contact.
- Use both a tone of voice and friendly expressions.
- Listen attentively and actively.
- Coordinate or synchronize your movements.
- Smile whenever the context is appropriate. It is one of the most positive emotional expressions; the brain prefers happy faces.

Measuring Organizational Social Intelligence

As you have noticed, being able to understand and identify SI an individual level is really essential to understanding where we are and what we are missing as we strive to reach our goals, both professionally and personally. When we talk about SI, we cannot overlook the same analysis at a collective level, whether in your personal, family or work environment.

Being able to know and understand the level of collective SI will be a very relevant process that will promote adjustment and improvement that must be undertaken to achieve common goal.

At the organizational level, it is important to be able to evaluate:

- The organizational image: how it looks, what is said about it, how it is projected.
- Internal communication: the effectiveness of the communication flow between colleagues, between leaders, between departments or divisions, between employees and clients.
- Performance in departments or teams: level of achievement or goals reached; fulfillment of deadlines; increase in sales, services, or recognitions.
- Organizational climate: work environment, dynamic between staff, service projection, among others.
- Continuous innovation: constant evaluation and measurement of processes, services, business lines, etc.

A very practical and precise exercise consists of using a satisfaction survey involving all the personnel of the organization so that they can offer their impression. This will allow the development of several premises so that people working in the organization can indicate their level of satisfaction. In this way, a process of analysis and development of strategies and activities can be initiated related to the areas of opportunity that align with the results.

Similarly, there are several tests to measure the level of SI in an organization. MindSonar® is a test developed by Dr. Jaap Hollander, Director of the Institute of Eclectic Psychology in Holland (Soto, n. d.). It is the most widely used because it allows the user to establish a specific context, which leads to a more accurate and personalized result for each participant.

The importance of knowing with precision and accuracy the level of SI of each collaborator will make a great contribution to the organization, considering that it saves time and money. This is because it makes it possible to attack in a direct, precise, and assertive way the areas that must be reinforced to reach the optimal organizational functioning.

This chapter has hopefully been very enriching; in fact, as I mentioned, EI, together with SI, is the backbone of my leadership proposal. But before I finish and move on to the next chapter, wherein we will deal with organizations and the elements that connect the leader with them, I would like to offer an exercise.

Suggested Exercise

Instructions: I would like to help you assess your developed EI skills. Answer the following questions, choosing from a scale of 1 to 5, according to how you identify yourself.

1. Never
2. Almost never
3. Occasionally
4. Almost always
5. Always

	Weighting
1. I am very sure about what I am passionate about in life.	
2. I must consult with others all the time to make decisions.	
3. I identify when I am starting to feel stress, I let it go and do not react.	
4. I do things impulsively, no matter with whom, because I can't keep those uncomfortable emotions.	
5. I understand their points of view and know what is going on with my peers.	
6. I accept myself as I am.	

7. I have a support group of friends, co-workers, family members or others.	
8. After I speak, I ask myself: why did I do it, I should have thought before speaking.	
9. I do not judge or point fingers at others, even if I do not agree with them.	
10. I admit that I was wrong and apologize.	
11. I spend time exercising, meditating, dancing, or some other activity.	
12. I can easily identify how the other person feels, through their nonverbal or verbal language.	
13. When I feel a strong emotion, I do not allow it to control me, I prefer to think of something else, a person or event from the past that generates good memories.	
14. I recognize when my mood is low, and I need to look for some method to increase my strength.	
15. I like to collaborate in a team.	
16. I say "no" easily.	
17. I choose my thoughts and do not get carried away by my emotions.	
18. I have the ability of active listening; I ask questions and understand others.	

19. I like to be recognized through awards, money, social acceptance, etc.	
20. I am aware of what I feel in my body (palpitations, aches, sweating, gestures) when I react emotionally.	
21. I am positive in the face of setbacks.	
22. I can persuade others with ease.	
23. I am a very compassionate person. I help others, recognizing what they need.	
24. I take the initiative without waiting for anything or anyone else.	
25. I am able to recognize when I need to take some time not to react inappropriately.	

Source: Bárbara Flores Caballero

Results

Next, write your score for each question in the corresponding EI skill. Add up the scores for each skill to obtain the result for that EI skill.

Self-knowledge	
Question number	Score
1	
6	
10	
16	
20	
Total	

Self-regulation	
Question number	Score
3	
13	
17	
21	
25	
Total	

Motivation	
Question number	Score
7	
11	
14	
19	
24	
Total	

Empathy	
Question number	Score
5	
9	
12	
18	
23	
Total	

Social skills	
Question number	Score
2	
4	
8	
15	
22	
Total	

Rating scale:

Acceptable: 25 -15.

Areas for improvement: 14-5.

Bullet points

- EI is a skill; therefore, it is learned.
- It is advisable to invest in EI training.
- A leader must have a very high EI.
- A leader must be self-aware and be able to self-regulate.
- Leaders must be motivated and have a motivated team.

- Empathy involves active listening and is an essential connector between people.
- Being empathetic means being compassionate and understanding, not complacent.
- A true leader trains their team of collaborators and future leaders.
- It is important that the leader offers a human, motivating, exemplifying, and inspiring response.
- The leader must direct emotions and the consequent motivation towards the achievement of objectives.
- A leader with a high level of SI takes others into account and thus enriches their interpersonal relationships.

Keywords

Emotional Intelligence · Empathy · Self-Awareness · Self-Regulation · Self-Realization · Intrinsic · Extrinsic Motivation · Automotivation · Empathy · Cognitive Empathy · Emotional Empathy · Compassionate Empathy · Social Ability · Emotions · Intellectual · Intellect · Human Leadership · Generation Z · Organizations · Profitability · Diversity · Baby Boomers · Centennial · Inspire · Influencing · Respect · Social Intelligence

Sources of information

Bar-On, R. (2000). Emotional and social intelligence. Insights from the emotional quotient inventory. In: R. Bar-On& J. D. Parker (Eds.). *The handbook of emotional intelligence: Theory, development assessment and application at home, school and in workplace.* Jossey-Bass.

Dilts, R. (2003). *El poder de la palabra: PNL* [The Power of Words: NLP (Neuro-Linguistic Programming)] Editorial Urano.

Essex, S. (2018). A brief history of social intelligence. Tracom. Retrieved from: https://n9.cl/i4o1v

Fisher, R. (2002). *Sí, de acuerdo (cómo negociar sin ceder).* [Getting to Yes: Negotiating Agreement Without Giving In]. Editorial Norma.

Gardner, H. (1999). *Intelligence reframed: Multiple intelligence for the 21st century*. Basic Books.

Goleman, D. (1996). *Inteligencia emocional* [Emotional Intelligence]. Kairós.

Goleman, D. (1998). *La inteligencia emocional en la empresa* [Emotional Intelligence in the Workplace]. Javier Vergara.

Goleman, D. (2006*). Inteligencia social: la nueva ciencia para mejorar las relaciones humanas* [Social Intelligence: The New Science of Human Relationships]. Barcelona, España: Editorial Planeta.

Goleman, D.,& Ekman, P. (2017). *Empathy*. Harvard Business Review.

Greenspan, S. (1989). *The essential partnership: how parents and children can meet the emotional challenges of infancy and childhood.* Viking Penguin.

Jacobson, E. (1987). Progressive relaxation. *The American Journal of Psychology, 100*(3/4), 522-537.

Krén, H., & Séllei, B. (2020). The role of emotional intelligence in organizational performance. In *Periodica Polytechnica Social and Management Sciences, 29*(1), 1-9.

Lim, G., & Hamid, N. (2021). The influence of emotional intelligence and coping strategies on employee productivity performance during Covid-19 pandemic. *Management of Technology and Business,2*(1), 485-498.

Maslow, A. (2013). *A theory of human motivation.* Martino Fine Books.

Menacho-Vargas, I., Jaramillo Ostos, D., Pérez Collantes, R., & Rivera Zamudio, J. (2022). *Influencia de la inteligencia emocional en el clima institucional en docentes de educación básica regular en épocas de Covid-19* [Influence of Emotional Intelligence on the Institutional Climate in Regular Basic Education Teachers During Covid-19 Times]. In *Archivos venezolanos de farmacología y terapéutica*, *41*(1), 52-57.

Payne, R. A. (2005). *Técnicas de relajación* [Relaxation Techniques]. Editorial Paidotribo.

Pérez, L. (2020). *Cómo aplicar la pirámide de Maslow para la motivación laboral.* [How to apply Maslow's Pyramid for Work Motivation]. UNIR, La Universidad en Internet. Retrieved from: https://www.unir.net/empresa/revista/como-aplicar-la-piramide-de-maslow-para-la-motivacion-laboral-de-tu-equipo/

Salovey, P., Woolery, A., & Mayer, J. (2001). Emotional intelligence: Conceptualization and measurement. In Fletcher, G. & Clark, M. S. (eds.). *Blackwell handbook of social psychology: Interpersonal processes* (pp. 279-307). Blackwell Publishers.

Scharrenberg, J. (2017). *Quién te enfada te controla* [Who make you angry controls you]. Sloyu Mindfulness. Retrieved from: https://n9.cl/qcpox.

Soto, L. (n.d.) *Los pensamientos, el lenguaje del cerebro* [Thoughts, the Language of the Brain]. Retrieved from: www.ligiasoto.com/mindsonar/.

CHAPTER 3:

HUMANIZED AND STRATEGIC LEADERSHIP

Customers respond positively to collaborators who are committed to the values of the organization and are passionate brand advocates.
Erick García

Three Stonemasons and One Mission[6]

The story goes that, in the Middle Ages, a pilgrim was traveling through Europe to reach Santiago de Compostela. On his way through Paris, he met a group of men who, in the middle of summer, at three o'clock in the afternoon and under an inclement sun, were working in a quarry cutting stones.

The pilgrim stopped to drink water and observed the hard work being performed by the stonemasons. Next to him stood one of them with a somber expression; he looked angry and wasted his energy by angrily hitting the rocks. The pilgrim asked him kindly:

"Sir, what is it that you are doing?"

The man answered grumpily, without even looking at his interlocutor and without stopping, hitting at the rock:

"Can't you see? Here I am, cutting stones under the sun since six o'clock in the morning. It's hard work, my back hurts, I'm thirsty and hungry. My work is very lame, I am a wretched man."

The pilgrim apologized shyly without daring to say anything more and continued walking. He stopped when he noticed another stonemason who was doing the same task as the previous one, but who did not seem so disgruntled. He was carrying out his work steadily and with apparent calm. The pilgrim, curious, turned to him and asked:

6 Taken from Caro, F. (2020). *Los tres canteros. La misión en las organizaciones* [The Three Stonemasons: Mission in Organizations]. Empresas de Comunicación.

“Sir, what are you doing?”

The man put down his mallet for a moment, wiped the sweat from his brow with his hand and, looking at the pilgrim without apparent emotion answered:

“Well, I make my living chopping stones, I have found no other trade to feed my family, I am glad to have this job.”

Catching his breath, he gave a slight smile and added:

“After all I’m not so bad. I am outdoors, I get to exercise, and there are certainly worse situations than mine.”

A little further on, there was a third stonemason. His attitude was totally different from that of the other two. He showed a frank smile and was pounding at the pile of stones with his mallet with enthusiasm and harmony. Such ardor was beautiful to see.

Intrigued, the pilgrim repeated the question:

“Sir, what is it that you are doing?”

The stonemason, smiling, stopped his work and put the mallet aside. Grateful for the stranger’s interest, he answered with excitement, drawing with his hands a great volume up in the air, and said:

“Me? I am building a cathedral, the Cathedral of Paris!”

Years later, the pilgrim had settled in Paris and went to visit the construction site of an important church. The project was in its infancy and the architect was still retouching the plans for what was to be a beautiful building. From a distance he recognized the architect as that stonemason who built cathedrals and who now, it seemed, was also designing them. He had thinned hair and many gray hairs, but he had not lost that glow that radiated the day the pilgrim met him pounding stones.

The pilgrim went over to talk to the stone mason and could see how, as he reviewed the plans that one of his assistants was finishing sketching, the former stonemason flew into a rage. Apparently, the asymmetrical position of a window offended the overall sense of the rear facade of the building. Then, the assistant, self-conscious, argued:

"Sir, that is no problem, the facade is part of an inner courtyard, and the window is so high that no one will be able to see it."

To which the architect replied:

"God can see it! We must fix it right now!"

After going through the eras of leadership and identifying with one of them, you moved on to working with your EI and SI. Now you will be able to recognize if your leadership aligns with the fundamentals of an organization in order to know if you want to work in it.

There have always been major companies, and I am not only referring to the image that today comes to our minds of a large corporate organization with work teams that assume different roles, but also to the "action or task that involves difficulty and whose execution requires decision and effort"[7]. In the case of this story you have just read,

---

7 (2022). Real Academia Española. Retrieved from: https://dle.rae.es/empresa

the enterprise was the construction of a great cathedral in which the three stonemasons are involved.

In turn, there is a mission with particular characteristics. One might ask: for what, for whom and how. If we look at it from a current standpoint, the mission (building a cathedral) constitutes one of the most permanent elements of the organization (the church) as we know it today, and this element is key to the behavior of all its members.

If leaders and collaborators consider that the mission of their organization goes beyond the achievement of economic profitability, motivation will be greater. This is what we see in the story. The first stonemason only notices this profitability, the second has a greater disposition, but the third is totally synchronized with the values of the organization in which he participates; he understands that the importance is not only material, but that it goes beyond. Can you see the importance of good foundations for an organization? Let's go deeper into this.

The Foundations of an Organization

When I refer to the foundations of an organization, I am talking about those fundamental bases that will allow its members to undertake the activities inherent to it in the right way in order to minimize errors in advance.

It is about establishing a solid structure that takes into consideration aspects such as purpose, vision, mission, values, and philosophy, from which, as a leader, you can act, focused on the objectives, without deviating from the path, and manage to unite all your collaborators around the achievement of the goals in favor of the organization (Delgado, 2003).

Purpose

The purpose of an organization is its permanent reason for existing. It is the reason why it exists and why its different actions are executed. This aspect is vital when making decisions, as it allows discernment between decisions that are correct and generate real value versus those that are simply easy or even technically eligible. In fact, a strategy by itself is not enough without a purpose.

The purpose of an organization is permanent, as long as it remains viable and finds a place in the reality it wishes to maintain. An organization is alive, so if at some point it is construed that the purpose must change because the organization wishes to pursue another goal, it must be clearly defined in order to redirect all resources.

People working together for a great purpose
do not have time to discuss trivial matters.
Rick Warren

As a leader with a defined purpose, it is important that you (Mendoza & Ortiz, 2006):

- Guide yourself and your team to bring out values, attitudes, and behaviors.

- Build your authority from your ability to connect in a genuine and profound way with your team.
- Be more intuitive and explore your human side.
- Be more resilient.

For example, when a business serves a customer, is the business truly acting out of service or just maximizing profits? Sam Walton, Walmart's founding leader, would answer immediately, because guided by altruism and compassion, he quickly focused on serving his customers. The purpose became clear and was quickly embraced by the entire organization. From the executive directors to the floor staff, everyone at Walmart is ready to serve the customer, which is everyone's top priority. *Let's look at other examples of purpose:*

Nurturing families so they
can flourish and thrive.
Kellogg's

Helping people manage risk and
recover from unexpected losses.
IAG

Organizing the world's information and
making it accessible to all.
Google

Vision

The vision, although not permanent as is the case with the purpose, is an aspect that is considered in the long term. A long term perspective speaks to a premise, the place you want to get to, in a specific period of time, through future plans, context, target audience and, of course, the vision itself.

In fact, vision takes into account the desire of the organization for how it will be in a few years, including possible changes. Of course, the customer or target audience is vital, so thinking about how to improve the lives of the customers in that context is also important.

The vision describes what kind of organization the entity wants to be, taking into consideration the purpose, in the long term, perhaps in a period of five to ten years, although this is not an upper limit and it can be even longer. Through the vision, it is possible to establish a defined direction for planning and executing corporate strategies.

> *Leaders create a vision with meaning, a relevant vision, which places all players at the center of things rather than on the periphery.*
> **Warren Bennis**

As a visionary leader, you must consider these aspects in order to develop organizational transformation strategies to achieve your objectives. In this sense, it is necessary to (Pérez, 2013):

- Promote innovation, learning, relationships, and creativity.
- Understand the motivation, inspiration and vision needs of your collaborators.
- Have clear and determined goals.
- Trust the scope of that goal, knowing that you can achieve it through all necessary strategies.

For example, innovation is an unquestionable part of Apple's vision; in this sense, Steve Jobs, as leader of this organization, stated the following:

> We believe we exist to make great products and we focus on innovation. We believe in the simple, not the complex. We believe we must control the technologies behind the products we make and participate only in markets where we can make a meaningful contribution. We believe in saying *no* to thousands of projects, so that we can really focus on the few that are truly important and meaningful to us.

It is clear that Apple is one of the companies that has achieved optimum results by adopting the right vision, according to its market niche.

Below, you will find other examples of organizational vision:

Leading the creation and delivery of innovative human capital solutions that enable our clients to succeed in the changing world of work.
Manpower

To be the most recognized Colombian brand in the world for its healthy growth and sustainable impact.
Juan Valdez

Our vision is to create innovative technology that is accessible to everyone and that adapts to the needs of each individual. Accessible technology eliminates barriers for people with disabilities and allows them to take full advantage of their capabilities.
Microsoft

Mission

When we talk about mission, we focus on what the organization does in a consistent manner to get closer to their vision. The purpose is the *why*, the mission is the *what*. A good mission should describe not only what the organization does, but also what it does not do. Both in the present as well as in the future, it should provide a focus for leaders and their collaborators.

A well-thought-out organizational mission should include timeliness in terms of vision and objectives, describe the business in which it operates, define the target audience or customer, and incorporate the metrics by which success is defined.

The "mission" is the heart of what is done as a team. Goals are simply steps toward its achievement. The "mission" has an external quality. Goals are time-limited and, once achieved, are replaced by others.
P. Dixon

As a leader, the mission is everything you consistently do with the goal of achieving the organization's vision. Therefore, it is also important that you:

- Inspire your collaborators to do what is expected of them optimally and on schedule.
- From the purpose, vision, values and philosophy of the organization, synchronize with the mission to lead the team to achieve the established objectives.
- Establish strategies and listen to your collaborators, who may have valuable contributions to the goal you are pursuing.

For example, with the presentation of Facebook's changes and transition to the Meta platform, Mark Zuckerberg, its founding leader and CEO, announced a new mission: "To give people the power to create communities and bring the world closer together."

Here are some examples of missions in organizations:

*Our mission defines the long-term objective
as a company and the right criteria
for actions and decisions to achieve three
fundamental goals: -Refresh the world.
-To inspire moments of optimism and happiness.
-Create value and make a difference.*
Coca-Cola

Inspire and develop the builders of tomorrow.
Lego

*Bringing inspiration and innovation
to every athlete in the world.*
Nike

Values

Values are the ethical and professional principles that evidence the organization's identity. They represent the personality of the organization, so they also guide decisions and behaviors by generating behaviors in line with what has been proposed.

*A brand for a company is like a reputation
for a person. You earn your reputation by trying
to do the hard things well.*
Jeff Bezos

Values also represent the focus and objectives that keep an organization active in the marketplace. In this sense, each one of the collaborators in the organization must be able to remember and apply them at all times. As a leader, with regard to values, it is necessary to (Irigoin & Vargas, 2002):

- Work as a team and with commitment.
- Articulate, model, and teach organizational values through actions.
- In addition, there must be a congruence between what distinguishes you as a leader and the values of the organization; this is essential.

If you lack these values, there will be no connection with the organization. You should also consider that these values generate credibility, contribute to the reduction of employee turnover by generating a solid organizational culture, improve the economic performance of the organization and facilitate the achievement of the objectives set.

A critical aspect would be to introspect and determine whether organizational values can be aligned with personal values. Personal values are a product of the process of upbringing, development, and maturity for each individual. Values should be considered, that what is important to one person is not necessarily important to another.

The fact that, as individuals, we can perform such introspection provides the power to confirm whether organizational values can be modeled through actions, behaviors, and continuous projection in their functions.

If there is no alignment at all with values, it is highly advisable to evaluate another place where you do not have to make a superlative effort to meet or, better yet, exceed in the projection of the defined values. Among the values that cannot be missing in an organization are the following (Da Silva, 2022):

- Honesty and transparency: because they generate trust.
- Passion: for the work, for customer service and for everything the organization says about it.
- Difference: what makes an organization and your team different from others.
- Customer orientation: because this is the central axis of a business.
- Quality: guarantee of the parameters established in the organization's niche.
- Social responsibility: this is a reflection of empathy, regardless of race, gender, age, class, religion, or political stance.

For example, from the founding of Amazon, its founding leader, Jeff Bezos, has put the customer first. In fact, he talks about being obsessed with it, going so far as to say: "Determine what your customers need and work from the end, backwards." In addition, operational excellence is a fundamental part of the organization, as is innovation. Below, I share some examples of the values held by different organizations:

Safety, collaboration, and creativity.
Adidas

Quality, accountability, togetherness, and improvement.
McDonald's

Commitment, usability, efficiency, and effectiveness.
McGraw-Hill Latin America

Philosophy

When we talk about philosophy within an organization, we understand that it as a set of principles and values that influences everything that surrounds it and guides all the decisions of the organization. Its purpose is to lay the foundations on which products and relationships will be built. The elements of organizational philosophy provide a rationale for its actions. Philosophy or rationale frames the reasons why you make one decision over another. It is an idea that encourages concrete action. From there on, it defines a path on which all plans and changes in a business converge.

Customers will never love a company
unless the employees love it first.
Simon Sinek

Organizational philosophy should be characterized by objectivity, simplicity, and relevance. Now, as a leader, you must ensure that the purpose is aligned with the products your organization sells, the services you provide and the way you want to position yourself in the market. In addition, it is important to take into account the organizational philosophy in order to[8]:

- Guide your team's actions.
- Create a sense of community around your brand.
- Attract ideal investors.
- Build a work team that is convinced of the organization's philosophy and, therefore, willing to apply it in their work.
- As the person responsible for hiring personnel, you must show congruence and choose employees who possess a profile compatible with the organization's code of ethics, in addition to their professional capacity.

Also, the leader must keep different individuals united with each other by conviction, by communion with the ideals of the organization, and by loyalty to the leader, the vision, and the mission they propose.

For example, the founding leader of Tesla and other well-known companies, Elon Musk, says the following:

8 (s. f.). *La congruencia del liderazgo con la filosofía empresarial.* [The congruence of leadership with business philosophy]. Pymex.

My driving philosophy is to expand the scope and scale of consciousness so that we can better understand the nature of the universe. I have a sort of proposed worldview or motivating philosophy, which is to understand what questions to ask about the answer, which is the universe.

Below, you will find examples of organizational philosophy:

Our values are passion, innovation, entrepreneurship spirit, open-mindedness, pursuit of excellence and accountability. Almost 15 years ago, we adopted an approach that focuses on ecological design in everything we do. In other words, we work continuously to reduce the environmental footprint of our products and improve their social impact.
L'Oréal

Offering high-quality products for all body types. This principle translates into the diversity of cuts, sizes, and colors of the pieces, in addition to the representativeness in the models who participate in the advertising campaigns.
Skims

Dedicate its talent and technology to create superior products and services that contribute to a

better global society. To achieve this, it sets a high value on its people and technologies.
Samsung

Differences Between Purpose, Vision, Mission, Values, and Philosophy

One of the most common mistakes with organizations is that many people mistake the mission and vision for the values of an organization. The truth is that, although they have some similarities, the three elements are complementary. The same goes for purpose and philosophy, they are different (Barraza, 2019).

Although these five aspects are different, none is more important than the other, they are all equally important. In fact, if your organization has these five foundations well established, it will be possible for you to make the right decisions, or at least help you redirect and refocus an issue for assertive decision making.

Organizational culture is composed of values, beliefs, assumptions, perceptions, rules, and behavior patterns common to all who work in the organization. Culture is to the organization what personality is to the individual: a hidden but unifying theme that provides meaning, direction and mobilization (Anzola, 2003).

The following establishes the differences between these aspects:

- Purpose: it is permanent.

- Vision: it is projected in the long term.
- Mission: is what you do constantly to get closer to the vision.
- Values: that which distinguishes you.
- Philosophy: beliefs that determine work dynamics.

Let's not lose sight of the most important factors that lead to successful leadership: commitment, a passion to make a difference, a vision to achieve positive change, and the courage for action.
Lorraine Matusak

Organizational Competencies

To continue a process of solidification in any organization, after establishing the foundations previously covered, it is necessary to ground them through organizational competencies. These competencies must be possessed or developed by all personnel or candidates who wish to join the organization in order to contribute to the achievement of the vision, mission and strategic objectives of the organization.

There are many organizational competencies; however, each organization must identify which are the most relevant, according to its business essence, its purpose and what it wishes to achieve. Certainly, it would seem to be easier to access the internet universe and do what is commonly known as "copy/paste." However, being able to responsibly dedicate time to analysis, as well as to focus on the integration of key people in the organization, becomes a significant return for the organization, strengthening ties and increasing the commitment of each member.

Likewise, organizational competencies can change over time as the organization faces changes, modifications or responds to external factors that directly impact the organization or its industry, leading them to adapt to the reality of the moment.

The exercise of defining the organization's competencies in a personalized way is what will differentiate it from other companies and help it stand out from others in the market. This process can be as simple or as complex as desired. If nothing is currently in place, it is best to start with something simple, but don't confuse simple with poor impact.

Starting with small steps, or baby steps, will pave the way for the organization to get used to and integrate new processes into its structure. Generally, this type of initiative is carried out with the help of an expert in the field to provide support and, at the same time, ensure that the process matures and capitalizes.

Taking small steps is a process that allows the identification of an internal resource person in the organization who possesses the preparation and experience to lead and promote the integration of other resources in an adequate manner. At the end of this chapter, you will find a practical exercise to evaluate this aspect.

A final aspect to consider is the continuity of everything we have discussed so far. You may have noticed that these processes involve time, effort, and investment of money.

Therefore, not providing continuity means throwing away what has been done. If the organization has a HR department or a professional expert in this area, it is highly likely that they can support the continuity process. Creating opportunities to ensure that every resource in the organization delivers value to all interested parties is an urgency that can be channeled through organizational leaders, supervisors, and HR professionals.

At a time when the labor market, projections, technology, emotional overload, and other external factors continue to threaten outcomes and success, organizations must strengthen their structures and ensure that their resources are reinforced with the necessary tools.

Increasingly, it is necessary to look closely and work with human capabilities; this means ensuring the right talent can meet strategic objectives, the culture links customer expectations with employee behaviors, leaders' actions generate trust and HR departments use an appropriate profile and practices. These human capabilities add value to customers, investors, and communities, not to mention they are difficult to copy (Ulrich, 2022).

Capitalization of Human Resources

A HR competencies and capabilities study conducted during the pandemic identified five competency domains for HR to deliver value and positivel impact in individual results, both for the interested parties and for the business. Each competency is described in the figure below.

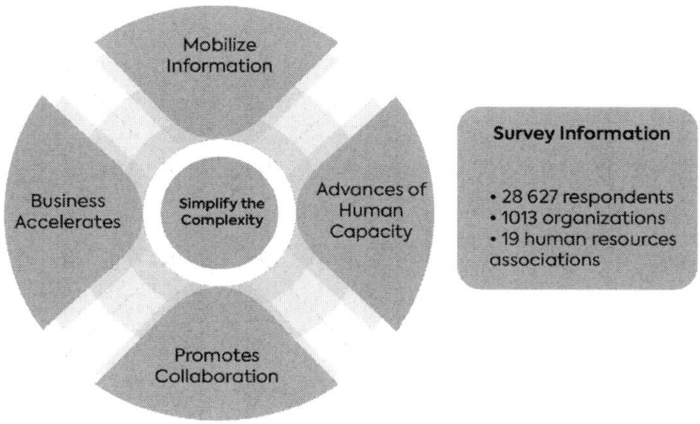

Source: HRD Connect.[9]

According to the model, to accelerate business results, HR must be active in conversations that are paramount to organizational success. This is because most of the issues that are often critical to an organization end up impacting the staff. This requires ensuring constant alignment in human capabilities, positioning, and results.

When HR maintains an active participation in key conversations, such as the value of intangibles, technological change, and regulations, among others, it helps an organization to succeed in the marketplace.

Improving human capabilities involves having a framework to understand the scope of all the aspects that

9 Dave Ulrich: 5 HR competencies (and actions) to enable renewal through human capability: https://n9.cl/ubb3xg.

must be aligned in key conversations and with the resources available to the organization.

Much of what is assessed directly impacts talent (e.g., human capital, competencies, work being performed), leadership (e.g., supervisors, hierarchy, senior management), and organization (e.g., teams, culture, processes). In the end, all these factors come into compliance with regulations and best practices in the field in order to add value.

Another competency is information mobilization. In this aspect, information must be provided to guide and prioritize investments in human capacity to ensure that they have the greatest impact on the organization's results.

Moreover, fostering collaboration is one of the fundamental pillars for success. Such collaboration must be fostered initially within each department, so that it can then be fostered across departments and at the organizational level. Promoting and maintaining the following key elements will help ensure positive relationships:

- Share a common purpose: results increase, and areas of opportunity or weaknesses are complemented when another possesses it as a strength.
- Respecting differences: greater gain is obtained when expressing and valuing a good performance vs. criticism for a bad one.
- Acceptance and connection: clearly define expectations so as not to create false illusions.
- Caring for relationship: show joy in the success of others and motivation in the face of failures, it has an im-

pact on the development and strengthening of the relationship.

- Sharing experiences: this is what enriches and nurtures the relationship.
- Collective growth: sharing meaning, learning from the past without getting stuck and focusing on what the future can be, is what allows moving in the same direction.

Finally, simplify complexity; that is to say, change complex choices into simple solutions through actions that show the organization's or leader's aspirations. Is the glass half full or half empty? It all depends on the level of thinking, and from which approach it is being interpreted.

It is the same with situations that, at first glance, may appear complex; however, if the discipline of simplicity is incorporated, knowledge can be produced by encouraging divergent thinking, which explores options, and then facilitating convergent thinking, which focuses on solutions. The leader's connection to the organization is very important to successfully lead their team in achieving the goals outlined here, as we have seen in this chapter. Throughout this book you have had at your disposal many practical tools; in the next chapter you will gain more, gathered according to all the content we have worked on and a little more.

Bullet points

- The purpose of an organization is permanent.
- The vision is set for the long term.
- The mission is what you constantly do to get closer to the vision.
- Values is what distinguishes you and it is essential.
- If you lack values, there will be no connection to the organization.
- Philosophy is the set of beliefs that mark the work dynamics.

Suggested Exercise

I share with you the following exercise that includes a step-by-step process, with the purpose breakoff breaking the ice and displaying an alternative very beneficial to the organization:

Step	Action	Observation
1	Ensure that the organization has a definition of its medium- and long-term vision, as well as the establishment of a defined strategic plan based on this vision.	This will help to have a clear map as to what you want to achieve.
2	Identify key people in the organization and create a work committee.	You may consider people who know the operation very well and who are a positive influence for others.
3	Conduct a dynamic of questions regarding what the members of the organization must possess and demonstrate in order to achieve the established goals.	It is important that what is identified can be projected through actions and behaviors.

4	Develop a specific definition of what it means for the organization, that which was identified in step 3.	One thing that may be identified is "teamwork." However, this goes beyond the definition that can be found in a dictionary. It means what is relevant to the organization, its structure, culture, among others.
5	Integrate competencies into other processes that have an impact on the organization to capitalize on them.	Some of the processes may be: recruitment of personnel, personnel development, performance evaluation, among others.
6	Inform the rest of the personnel.	There is no point in identifying competencies if they are not shared with those who must ensure their implementation.
7	Continually assess the relevance and pertinence of competencies.	The organization is alive, so competencies may be impacted.

Source: Saraí González Berríos

Keywords

Organizational Competencies · Purpose · Vision · Mission · Values · Beliefs · Lead · Organizational culture · Organizational philosophy

Sources of information

Anzola, O. (2003). *Una mirada a la cultura corporativa* [A look at corporate culture]. Universidad Externado de Colombia.

Barraza, H. (2019). *¿Cuál es la diferencia entre propósito, misión y visión de una organización?* [What is the difference between purpose, mission, and vision of an organization?]. Ayse Lucus. Retrieved from: https://n9.cl/4ywzyv.

Da Silva, D. (2022). *Valores de una organización.* [Values of an organization]. Retrieved from: https://n9.cl/by9dw.

Delgado, N., & Delgado, D. (2003). *El líder y el liderazgo: reflexiones* [The leader and the leadership: reflexions]. In *Revista Interamericana de Bibliotecología, 26*(2),75-88. Universidad de Antioquia.

Irigoin, M., & Vargas, F. (2002). *Competencia laboral: manual de conceptos, métodos y aplicaciones en el sector salud* [Work Competence: Manual of Concepts, Methods, and Applications in the Health Sector]. Cinterfor-OPS.

Mendoza, M., & Ortiz, C. (2006). *El liderazgo transformacional, dimensiones e impacto en la cultura organi-*

zacional y eficacia de las empresas [Transformational Leadership: Dimensions and Impact on Organizational Culture and Business Effectiveness]. In *Revista Facultad de Ciencias Económicas: Investigación y Reflexión*, *XIV*(1), 118-134. Universidad Militar Nueva Granada.

Pérez, R. (2013). *Liderazgo visionario: centro del conocimiento* [Visionary Leadership: Center of Knowledge]. In *Revista EAN,* (58), 79-86.

Ulrich, D. (28 de febrero de 2022). *5 competencias (y acciones) de recursos humanos para permitir la renovación a través de la capacidad humana* [5 HR competencies (and actions) to enable renewal through human capability]. HRD Connect. https://n9.cl/ubb3xg.

CHAPTER 4:

TOOLS FOR SUPPORT AND CONTINUITY

The magnitude of a leader is given by the depth of its convictions, the degree of its ambitions, the angle of its vision and the scope of its love.

D. N. Jackson

Water and Fire[10]

In the 4th century B.C., hidden within the state of Lu, was a district ruled by Duke Chuang. The place, though small, had prospered remarkably in the time of Chuang's predecessor, but ever since his appointment to the position, its affairs had deteriorated considerably. Surprised by the sad turn of events, Chuang went to the mountain seeking the wisdom of the great master Mu-sun.

When the duke arrived at the mountain, he found the great master sitting quietly on a small rock, looking out over the valley. After the duke had explained his situation to Mu-sun, he waited holding his breath for the great master to speak. However, contrary to Chuang's expectation, the master whispered not even a word. Instead, he smiled softly and with a gesture he signaled the duke to follow him.

They walked in silence until they found the Tan Fu River before them, the end of which could not be seen because it was so long and wide. After meditating on the river, Mu-sun set about to light a fire. When he had lit it and the flames were blazing, the master asked Chuang to sit beside him.

They sat for endless hours as the fire glowed in the night. Upon the brink of the new day, when the flames were no longer dancing, Mu-sun pointed to the river. Then, for the first time since the duke's arrival, the grandmaster spoke:

---

10 Taken from: Path MBA. Parábolas del liderazgo [Parables of Leadership].

"Now do you understand why you are unable to do what your predecessor did: maintain the greatness of your district."

Chuang looked at him perplexed; he really did not understand any more than before. With great embarrassment he said:

"Great master, forgive my ignorance, for I cannot comprehend the wisdom you are imparting."

Then Mu-sun spoke a second time:

"Chuang, reflect on the nature of the fire that burned before us last night. It was strong and powerful. Its flames leaped as if dancing and shouted with boastful pride. Neither strong trees nor wild beasts could match its strength. With ease, it could have conquered everything in its path. Instead, think of the river. It begins as a small stream in the distant mountains. Sometimes it flows slowly, sometimes swiftly, but it always glides downward, accepting the lowlands to follow its course. It gladly penetrates every crevice of the land and willingly fills every dent. Nature is as humble as this. When we listen to the water it can hardly be heard. When we touch it, it can hardly be felt, its nature is very gentle. Yet, in the end, what is left of what was once a mighty fire? Barely a handful of ashes, for the fire is so strong, Chuang, that it not only destroys everything in its path, but eventually falls victim to its own strength and is consumed. The same is not true of the quiet river. Just as it always was, it is now, and always will be flowing eternally, growing deeper, wider, ever more powerful on its journey to the unfathomable ocean, providing life and sustenance for all."

After a moment of silence, Mu-sun turned to the duke and continued:

"Just as in nature, Chuang, it is the same with rulers. For it is not fire, but water that envelops all and which is the source of life. It is not the powerful and authoritarian rulers, but the humble rulers who with an inner strength that goes deep within, the ones who conquer the hearts of the people who are the source of prosperity for their states. Ponder, Chuang, on the kind of ruler you are. It is possible that the answer you are looking for is found therein."

And as if a flash of lightning had struck, the truth seized the duke's heart. He no longer felt proud, but troubled and uncertain. However, he looked up with enlightened eyes. Chuang could no longer see anything but the sun rising over the river.

As with Duke Chuang, from the story you have just read, it is possible that after having come this far you are not entirely clear about what kind of leader you are, or perhaps you do know, but you understand that you can always learn more and enrich your own leadership. Be it one way or another, the interesting thing is that you can confirm or identify your leadership style to reinforce or acquire the necessary tools and skills to be a better leader every day. Precisely, that is the objective of this chapter.

Self-awareness, Self-consciousness and Self-reflection

As a leader, you need to be aware of how your habits, behaviors, decisions, and views impact your team in positive ways, but also negative ways. This is why reflecting on your leadership frequently can be an incredible way to stay connected with your own management and with your collaborators. Take into consideration that to become a more effective leader you must have the right tools, related to self-knowledge, that lead you to reflect on how your unique characteristics also affect the achievement of the objectives of your organization (Mendoza, 2014).

Knowing thyself, that is the greatest wisdom.
Galileo Galilei

The central idea at this point is for you to be aware of yourself, to know yourself as well as possible and thus be able to actively reflect and ponder how other people perceive your words and actions so that you can focus on, among other things, working to address your shortcomings. Remember that as a leader your first objective is to lead your people more effectively. This is how we can talk about self-awareness and self-reflection (Mackey, 2019), qualities that are really important for a good leader because:

- They help you make better decisions.
- They facilitate the understanding of what is brought into this role.

- They allow you to understand your strengths in both technical skills and knowledge, as well as in your personal characteristics to better perform your responsibilities within the organization.
- They help you to be realistic in your expectations.
- They encourage you to raise your level of EI, including greater empathy for others.

A truly self-aware leader is reflective, observant, empathetic, perceptive, sensitive, humble, able to self-regulate, and discern as well as being able to adapt. They possesses the capacity for self-evaluation. We must not forget that for a leader to build a team, there is a need to act in a shared sense, meaning based on a shared vision (Senge, 2007). To achieve this, it is necessary that this introspective process takes place.

Self-reflection is the school of wisdom.
Baltasar Gracián

Self-evaluation

Nowadays, it is possible to carry out a self-assessment or evaluation of your leadership, considering that it is measurable; therefore, it is possible to carry out an assessment of the style and skills of an individual in their role as a leader. As a methodology, it is possible to use various tests and analyses that allow you to determine your strengths and management potential.

Of course, there are different approaches, but most tend to assess both the personality traits inherent in a leader as well as their responses and skills in specific situations. The truth is that whichever instrument or method you use, you must keep the following in mind:

- They can increase your self-awareness.
- They are capable of guiding you in the creation of your professional goals.
- They may help improve your leadership development plan.
- They can help you improve at every stage of your career.

Practice 1

Before moving on, let's review the concepts related to positive leadership that are vital to your performance as a leader.

Below, you will find a table with different key concepts within leadership that we have been reviewing chapter by chapter. You must match the correct pairs from each column, the meaning that corresponds to each word or phrase in the left column, as indicated in the example (i.e., the two shaded boxes):

Table 1. *Tools for Concept Evaluation*

Mission	This leader assumes full responsibility in decision making and may even impose force in order to achieve objectives.
Types of empathy according to Goleman and Paul Ekman	Ability to perceive and express emotions, to assimilate emotions into thought, to understand and reason with emotions, and to regulate emotions in oneself and others.

Elements of EI	1. Identify thoughts. 2. Manage thoughts since these come before the emotion. 3. Knowing how to identify emotions. 4. Manage emotions. 5. To watch over its conduct and behavior.
Factors of EI	That which you constantly do to get closer to the vision.
Transformational leadership	That which distinguishes you as a leader and is essential.
Social Intelligence (SI) according to Goleman	A person's ability to recognize the emotions of others, meaning, the ability to understand the feelings of others and to be able to read their nonverbal messages.
Empathy	The purpose, vision, mission, values, and philosophy.
Autocratic leadership	Leadership model characterized by inspiration and motivation on the part of the leader, as well as on the part of the leader to its team.

Philosophy	Self-awareness, self-regulation, motivation, empathy, and social skills.
Emotional Intelligence (EI)	Cognitive, emotional, and compassionate
Fundamentals of an organization	This ability allows us to capture other people's moods, feelings, motivations, and fears almost instantaneously, as well as to interact with them effectively.
Values	Set of beliefs that mark the work dynamics.

Source: Bárbara Flores Caballero

Self-Assessment Tools

Based on your self-knowledge, self-awareness, and self-reflection, it is possible for you to implement a self-assessment plan that will bring about the above-mentioned benefits. There are several leadership assessment tools that allow you to identify your potential talent (Ortega, n. d.), in addition to reinforcing some ideas about yourself that you may already know. In the following table you will find three options, although, there are many, as I mentioned before:

Table 2. *Comparative table of leadership self-evaluation tools*

Test	Focus	Utility	Features
Gallup Strengthfinder Test	Strengths rather than weaknesses, preferences, or behaviors.	Helps create a more positive mindset from information that can be very useful in improving leadership skills.	At the end of the evaluation, you learn which five strengths among a list of thirty possibilities you most strongly possess.
360-degree Feedback	Perception of third parties within the work environment.	Helps identify any recurring leadership trend.	It involves receiving comments from several colleagues, whether anonymously or not.

Goldstein Auto-test	Social skills.	Helps you identify your self-perception about your social skills in order to continuously improve in this aspect.	You get a quantitative assessment, based on a scale of social skills classified in different groups.
MindSonar® Test	Thoughts in an established context.	Helps in knowing and analyzing styles of thinking, provides a great opportunity to be more effective and work the areas of opportunity aligning them to the needs of the position and/or company.	It allows you to know how a person thinks in a particular scenario, which is represented in fifteen metaprograms.

Source: Bárbara Flores Caballero

Implementing a self-assessment of this type is ideal for measuring the competencies of an effective leader, because these self-assessments go beyond the specific skills of each function, considering also measures of personality traits —depending on the type of instrument— and the skills necessary to exercise a leadership role.

Being entirely honest with oneself is a good exercise.
Sigmund Freud

Now, among these four options, I would like to introduce you to an assessment instrument based on Goldstein's Auto-test (Andújar Orientation, 2018). However, I would first like to go a bit deeper regarding social skills, considering that this assessment is based on such skills.

As I mentioned in the second chapter, EI and SI are fundamental in the current leadership context. In this sense, it is very important to understand that social skills are the channel through which we relate to other people. As they are a set of skills, some general and others specific, it is possible to develop them, even learn them from the ground up. This is vital for a leader, understanding that there are tools that allow us to establish contacts and express attitudes, desires, opinions, rights, and feelings in an assertive way. Examples of these skills are the ability to listen, engage in conversation, ask questions, say thank you, know how to present oneself correctly, introduce others, praise, empathize, define problems, seek solutions, negotiate, and apologize, among others.

Now that you've learned more, it's time to practice.

Practice 2

Instructions: Below, you will find 25 social skills classified in six groups. Evaluate, scoring from 1 to 5, each of your skills, understanding that 1 is the lowest score and 5 is excellent.

Social Skills Self-Assessment Instrument

Group	Skill	Weighting
Group 1 First social skills	Initiate a conversation	
	Say thank you	
	Listening	
	Pay a compliment	
	Introducing oneself	

Group	Skill	Weighting
Group 2 Advanced social skills	Giving instructions	
	Apologizing	
	Convince other people	
	Follow instructions	
	Ask for something	
Group 3 Skills related to feelings	Expressing affection	
	Knowing one's own feelings	
	Understand the feelings others	
	Dealing with other people's anger	
	Self-rewarding	

Group	Skill	Weighting
Group 4 Alternative skills to aggression	Negotiate	
	Avoid uncomfortable situations with other people	
	Asking permission	
	Defending one's rights	
	Self-regulate	

Group	Skill	Weighting
Group 5 Stress management skills	Responding to persuasion	
	Formulating a complaint	
	Preparing for a difficult conversation	
	Coping with group pressures	
	Responding to failure	

Group 6 Planning skills		
	Establish an objective	
	Take initiatives	
	Make a decision	
	Collect information	
	Knowing one's own skills	
Total		

Source: Bárbara Flores Caballero
(based on Goldstein's Auto-test)

Results: Once you have completed the weighting of each of the items in the social skills groups, proceed to add up all the points and divide the total by 30 (which is the total number of items evaluated). The result will be the average of the exercise in its entirety. In this way, you will have a fairly accurate outline of your self-perception regarding your social skills and, therefore, it will be possible for you to draw a road map that will lead you to the continuous improvement of these skills.

If your average score was 4 or 5, your social skills capacity is very good, which makes it easier for you to exercise those skills that still present opportunities. If, however, your score is 3, you are halfway through the development process in the aspects to be improved. And if the average result is 1 or 2, you may need a significant reinforcement throughout the whole set of these social competencies.

Another way to interpret your results is to calculate the average for each of the groups. In this way, you will be able to extract opportunities for improvement in those areas where you scored 3 or below.

Leadership Tools

Throughout the pages of this book, you have been learning and reinforcing concepts regarding leadership, as well as the various necessary elements for successful management not only for the leader, but for your team and the organization. It is now clear to you that to be a good leader it is not enough to focus on superficial aspects, but also on emotional elements, among others.

Leadership is not only limited to doing a good job, it also involves having the ability to motivate and inspire others to follow the path you have set to achieve the organization's objectives, without neglecting the interests of collaborators.

Leaders will be those who empower others.
Bill Gates

As I mentioned at the beginning, a leader is born and made, so you need to acquire tools through learning. I have mentioned many of them, but I would like to reinforce them, so that you can put them into practice. Remember that to achieve good leadership it is key to integrate habits, implement best practices and connect with your people.

1. EI: This tool, which can be developed, involves concepts such as empathy and the ability to understand the needs and desires of others. How to put it into practice:

- Learn the names of your collaborators and always communicate with each of them using their names.
- Be empathetic when they express an inconvenience that prevents them from coming to the office, be available and offer them help to the best of your ability.
- Support collaborators from other generations as much as possible.

2. Kindness and respect: Both are key elements in leadership. One does not exist without the other. These are basic elements of leadership that should never be lost. How to put it into practice:

- When you arrive at your workplace, greet every member of your team every day.
- Be communicative in an assertive way, do not complain aggressively, but ask politely the details of something that did not go as expected in order to correct it properly, without your collaborators feeling mistreated.
- Listening attentively is synonymous with respect. This is what is called active listening.

3. Continuous learning: Even if you are a leader, this does not imply that you are a wiser person; in fact, there are always things to learn. It is advisable that you keep awakening your curiosity and desire to continue evolving in a positive direction. How to put it into practice:

- Sign up for workshops, courses, specializations in your area, but also in leadership programs that involve aspects such as EI and SI.
- Read. There is a lot of literature focused on leadership, project management, coaching, mentoring, whatever your area of expertise; take advantage of this invaluable resource for your training.
- Sign up for newsletters from online sites focused on leadership and management, such as *Forbes Magazine* or LinkedIn.

4. Do not control: Leadership is influence, guidance, and support, but not control. Great leaders inspire and then let people fly on their own. How to put it into practice:

- Avoid constant monitoring of your team and micro-management; trust the results you get from them.
- If possible, implement a hybrid model; for example, a combination of on-site and remote. This gives confidence and freedom to your collaborators, who are aware of their work and the results you are all looking for together.
- Allow your collaborators to organize themselves, that is, to self-manage the team through their own agreements.

5. Contextualize: By this I mean being able to identify different situations with their characteristics and moments. Take into account that it is possible that what once worked wonderfully may lead to failure in another context. How to put it into practice:

- Analyze those situations which bring about the same results a high percentage of the time and evaluate why. Understanding the context will allow you to manage your own procedures manual in this regard.
- Likewise, study why certain situations have been complicated; it is important to understand the factors that led to unexpected results.
- Evaluate the time, place, time of year, time of day, people involved, methodologies, resources, etc., of

situations that have yielded both positive and negative results.

6. Collaboration: Never stop getting involved with your collaborators, take into account that if you follow this path, the probabilities that the results will be surprising will increase, even for you. How to put it into practice:

- Know in detail the work involved in the role of each collaborator.
- Think about which tools would facilitate your team's process.
- Work on intellectual stimulation, taking into account that "increased capabilities and commitments presumably result in extra effort and more productivity" (Leithwood, 2004). Encourage the training and updating of your collaborators, as well as your own.

7. Care about others: In addition to your performance as a leader at the administrative level, it is important that you know what your collaborators goals are so that you can help them achieve them to the best of your ability. This will help you to make them feel at ease, which, in turn, generates greater productivity. How to put it into practice:

- Sit down periodically with your collaborators.
- Try to get to know the personal context of your collaborators, without being invasive. Maybe one of their relatives is sick or they are making an effort to pay for their studies, and you could help them.

- Keep an agenda of the birthdays of your team members, it may seem simple, but it is a small detail that makes them feel taken into account and, therefore, they will feel at ease.

8. Honesty: It is really necessary that the leader transmits credibility. Otherwise, leadership will not work at all. How to put it into practice:

- Be completely transparent about both the strengths and virtues of your team when praising or calling attention to them.
- Transmit what you are really willing to do; do not deceive your collaborators by offering things that you will not be able to accomplish.
- Never lie.

Effective leadership is not about making speeches or being liked; leadership is defined by results.
Peter Drucker

The Ideal Leader

The universal ideal leader does not exist; that is, there is no one leadership style that is perfect for absolutely every organization or the development of the talent of all the members of every team (García, 2020). Just as there is no magic formula that will make you a leader by chance. As has already been made clear, in order to become the good leader that your team and your organization need, you must make an effort, gain knowledge and, above all, pursue self-knowledge, as we learned at the beginning.

You must consider that you have a unique personality with particular characteristics and innate skills, talents and also weaknesses. Yes, certainly the universal ideal leader does not exist, but you can be the one that you, your team and your organization require. This is a decision that only you can make. Therefore, I would like to introduce you to a new practice, described below.

Practice 3

Instructions: Here is a new questionnaire, a self-assessment tool that you should answer as honestly as possible.

1. After learning about the characteristics of a self-aware, positive, and emotionally intelligent leader, what do you feel you need to improve in every sense?

2. After having performed several self-assessment exercises, where are you located right now as a leader and which path are you taking?

Source: Bárbara Flores Caballero

Recommendations for Tools, Programs and Training

Developing skills and improving those aspects you have already detected is possible through learning new knowledge. That is why I would like to make some recommendations that may work as a guide for you.

Supervision Resources

Let's measure your level of supervisory knowledge. The time has come to exercise a supervisory and leadership role through which you can raise your level of performance and that of your work team, where you will achieve the following:

- Be recognized as a leader who exceeds results.
- Eliminate stress and provoke high performance in your team.
- Increase commitment and turn your collaborators into your best allies.
- Generate assertive and impactful conversations.
- Demonstrate high skills while interviewing, evaluating, developing, motivating, researching, and even disciplining.

Assertive Supervision Test (only avaliable in spanish)
Test your level of knowledge as a supervisor by taking this short survey: https://forms.gle/fxiPX-22hJxaC53UQ9.

Assertive Supervision Certification
Get certified as an assertive supervisor. Become a supervisor who is proficient in the essential roles for executing and delivering results. Visit the link: https://n9.cl/k804z.

Human Resources and Supervisory Training

You can get access to the tools of the Academy for training in HR and supervision at the following link (only avaliable in spanish): https://assertiveacademy.com/

Bullet points

- As a leader, you need to be aware of how your habits, behaviors, decisions, and views impact your team.
- A truly self-aware leader is self-reflective.
- A leader possesses the ability to self-evaluate based on self-knowledge, self-awareness, and self-reflection.
- Social skills are the channel through which we relate to other people.
- Leadership also involves the ability to motivate and inspire others.

Keywords

Self-Awareness · Self-Reflection · Leadership Tools · Training · Self-Assessment · Gallup Test · 360 Degree · Feedback · Goldstein Auto-Test · Social Skills · Emotional Intelligence · Empathy · Ideal Leader · Supervision Resources · Human Resources · Certification

Sources of information

Colombo, D. (2022). *Autotest para medir las habilidades sociales con estos 50 indicadores de Goldstein* [Self-test to measure social skills with these 50 Goldstein indicators]. Forbes. Retrieved from: https://n9.cl/4p8gm.

García, J. (2020). *El líder ideal no existe* [The ideal leader does not exist]. Equipo humano. Retrieved from: https://n9.cl/v20cw.

Leithwood, K. (2004). *El liderazgo con éxito. El liderazgo educacional transformador en un mundo de políticas transaccionales.* [Successful leadership. Transformative educational leadership in a world of transactional politics].

Villa, A. (coord.). Dirección para la innovación: apertura de los centros a la sociedad del conocimiento. IV Congreso Internacional sobre Dirección de Centros Educativos. ICE Universidad de Deusto.

LHH. (2022). La importancia de la autoconciencia en el liderazgo [The importance of self-awareness in leadership]. Spring Professional. Retrieved from: https://n9.cl/3dret.

Mackey, Z. (2019). *Los líderes, rompen la autodecepción con la autorreflexión* [Leaders break through self-deception with self-reflection]. Arbinger Institute. Retrieved from: https://n9.cl/791m9.

Mendoza, X. (2014). *Mejorando el liderazgo directivo a partir de la autorreflexión de actuaciones directivas en una universidad mexicana en contexto de cambio. El Caso del Bachillerato Politécnico* [Improving managerial leadership through self-reflection of managerial actions in a Mexican university in a context of change. The Case of the Polytechnic Baccalaureate]. *Paulo Freire Revista de Pedagogía Crítica, 13*(16),89-103. https://n9.cl/ egb88.

Orientación Andújar. (2018). *Test escala cuestionario de habilidades sociales editable* [Editable social skills questionnaire scale test]. Retrieved from: https:// n9.cl/zuqny.

Ortega, C. (n. d.). *Evaluación del liderazgo. Qué es y herramientas para realizarla* [Leadership assessment. What it is and tools to perform it]. Question pro. Retrieved from: https://n9.cl/b5x00.

Senge, P. (2007). *La quinta disciplina. El arte y la práctica de la organización abierta al aprendizaje* [The Fifth Discipline: The Art and Practice of the Learning Organization]. Granica.

EPILOGUE

Before you are a leader, success is all about growing yourself. When you become a leader, success is all about growing others.
Jack Welch

Flight of the Geese[11]

In early autumn, a grandfather was walking with his grandson in his garden. They were looking at the sky when the boy asked him:

"Grandpa, why are those birds flying like that? It looks like an incomplete triangle."

The grandfather smiled and said:

"You see, dear grandson, every fall, when you see the geese heading south for the winter, notice that they fly in a V shape or an incomplete triangle, as you said. As you can see, science has discovered why some birds fly this way."

"And what does science say?" asked the boy in amazement.

"Scientists have studied birds and have found that when each bird flaps its wings, it produces a movement in the air that helps the bird behind it."

"Because they are friends, Grandpa!" said the little boy excitedly.

11 Based on Stories for Leaders: *El vuelo de los gansos* [The flight of geese] by Daniel Colombo.

“Yes! Because flying in a V, like those geese,” he said, pointing to the sky., “The whole flock increases its power by at least 71%, and that’s a lot, far beyond what each bird would achieve if it flew alone.”

“How does the 71% power come about?” asked the boy doubtfully.

”The power that all living beings have in every activity or action, such as running, flying, walking, is 100%, and it is our maximum. It varies from one person to another, from one living being to another. As you can see, 71% is pretty close to 100 %. That’s a lot of power when all those geese are together.”

“Grandpa, is that why I can make block houses faster when I am with my friends than when I am alone?”

“Exactly, dear grandson!” The Grandpa commented excitedly, “That is exactly what I wanted to explain to you. Did you know that it has been proven that people who unite and share a common path get where they want to go faster and easier because they support and strengthen each other?”

“You mean we have more power together?” asked the boy.

“Yes, exactly. Every time a goose goes out of formation, it immediately feels the resistance of the wind, at that moment it realizes the difficulty of doing it alone and quickly returns to the formation to benefit from the power of those ahead and help those behind. Now imagine if we acted with the intelligence of geese, we would do our best to overcome differences, share the same direction and serve with the best of ourselves."

"We can be like geese and help each other"! said the excited boy. "Of course! They have a leader, the one at the tip," the boy said, pointing at the top of the flock. The one at the front."

"Yes, the leader," Grandpa smiled. "More than a boss, he is a leader, he doesn't command over the others, but takes responsibility and guides the others, working as a team. When he gets tired of flapping his wings, then he moves to one of the back positions and another goose takes his place. So can we, because we always get better results if we take turns doing the more difficult jobs, rather than allowing the burden to be carried by a few or just one."

"So, all the geese are leaders?" asked the boy.

"Each one of them, at the right time, collaborates with each other in order to reach the south, their destination. It is not cold over there at this time of year, and they can all survive the winter together."

"I want to be a leader, Grandpa," said the boy.

"You already are. You help your little friends and together they achieve their goals. You propose ideas and accept theirs when it's more convenient. Of course, dear grandson, you can always be a better leader."

Indeed, biologists have observed that the geese that are behind produce a particular sound to encourage those in front to keep up their speed. In our case, a word of encouragement produces great benefits. The encouragement motivates and comforts.

In addition, when a goose becomes ill or is wounded due to a gunshot, two others leave the formation to follow it with the intention of helping and protecting it. They stay with this goose, accompanying it, until it is fit to fly again or until it dies. Only then do the two companions return to their flock or join another group.

If we learn from the geese how to be in solidarity with those who need us and stay with each other, accompanying and supporting each other, the path will be easier and lighter for everyone. A genuine leader manages to establish this bond with their collaborators; they know that it is not about themselves, but about the multiple factors that we have seen in this book. Now that you have more tools and knowledge to optimize your leadership, it's time to put it into action!

The difference between the boss and the leader is that the boss says "go" and the leader says, "let's go."
E. M. Kelly

Printed in Great Britain
by Amazon

48114976R10110